ONCE UPON A TIME

A Humorous Re-telling of The Genesis Stories

W. J. A. POWER

Illustrations by Anne Coke

ABINGDON PRESS
Nashville

ONCE UPON A TIME

Copyright © 1992 by Abingdon Press

All rights reserved.

This book is printed on recycled, acid-free paper.

Library of Congress Cataloging-in-Publication Data

POWER, W. J. A., 1935-
  [Book of Genesis]
  Once upon a time : a humorous retelling of the Genesis stories / W. J. A. Power.
    p.   cm.
  Originally published under title The book of Genesis and appeared in The Perkins School of Theology journal, winter 1984.
  ISBN 0-687-28849-5 (alk. paper)
    1. Bible stories, English—O.T. Genesis. 2. J document (Biblical criticism) I. title.
  BS550.2.P684   1992
  222'.1109505—dc20   91-23788
                                                                          CIP

MANUFACTURED IN THE UNITED STATES OF AMERICA

ONCE UPON A TIME

For
Punkin
Elizabeth
Emily
and Sarah.
Each of whom has taught me more about life
and its Giver,
than I would ever have anticipated.

Contents

Introduction.. 9

Part I   Once Upon a Time.................... 15

Part II   Abram: An Average Man.......... 29

Part III   God's Chosen People:
                A Caricature............................52

Part IV   Joseph: Man Proposes, God
                Disposes..................................... 71

Introduction

This is a collection of stories. It is not a work of systematic or philosophical theology, of ethics or of law. It is, rather, a retelling of some extraordinary tales, so durable and so viable that they have been told for thousands of years, and have served as the inspiration for much of the theology, ethics, and law that Jews and Christians have written. Through these stories humans have sensed more profoundly where the meaning of life is to be found. Through them they have learned something about themselves, and have gained as well at least a glimpse of who God is. On the truths conveyed by them, three religions have built their tenets of faith and their way of life. Amongst Jews and Christians, it has become a fundamental tradition to tell and retell, to interpret and to reinterpret these stories, which from ancient times have been the conveyors of the faith. This collection attempts to continue that tradition.

The story-telling tradition is the oldest means of communicating human religious understanding, and probably the most effective. Jesus used the same technique when he taught through parables. And the early church continued the tradition by relating stories about Jesus and about his disciples. Down through the centuries rabbis have told more tales to interpret the basic core of the biblical narrative. Christian clergy, standing in the same tradition, use stories to illustrate their sermons, and it is usually the picture language of the story that listeners of all ages remember long after the abstractions have been forgotten. No doubt, it is easier for all of us to participate in the drama of a good story than it is for us to appropriate codes of ethics and laws or theological treaties. In any case, Jews and Christians, concerned to express their faith, have from earliest times used stories to convey their message to others more effectively.

In ancient times the stories that we have in our Bible were transmitted orally from one generation to the next and from one group of people to another. The Hebrews told stories that were originally developed amongst their own people, and they also told stories that they heard from their Egyptian and Babylonian neighbors. Lacking books, radio, and television, the Hebrews, like all ancient people, used story telling as a means of entertainment around the campfire, at the gate, or at the well, or wherever people might gather. But the stories with which we are dealing were not told merely to entertain. They were used as well in a variety of religious settings as vehicles through which the Hebrews reminded one another, and also taught their children their understanding of who God is, who they were as humans, and what the meaning of life was. The stories were, in contemporary terms, teaching-learning devices. That they were inherently entertaining rather than didactic, rendered them, as modern educators are aware, all the more effective. Indeed, their entertainment value in part explains their vitality and their longevity. Because they are not philosophical, systematic, or didactic statements, each person who hears them can assimilate them by participating in them through identifying with the characters in the tale. One may then make one's own comment upon the story, just as countless theologians, ethicists, and legalists have done. Because of their form these stories invite comment. One might almost say that they *demand* comment from every generation that hears them, and most assuredly they will continue to make their insistent demand on future generations as long as the Book and the Tradition survive. Moreover, as long as they exist, they will continue to be available as both an inspiration to and a check on our attempts at being theologians. But the story-telling method of communicating religious truths allows for contemporary adaptation without violating the truths themselves. And the corollary of that statement is that the veracity of the stories does not, therefore, depend upon their historical accuracy.

10

For over two centuries now the Book of Genesis has been subjected to close literary analysis. That process is by no means complete today. Indeed, it is doubtful if it ever will be brought to a satisfactory completion. As things stand, many scholars are persuaded that the Book of Genesis is the product of the editorial work of a Jewish editor who compiled it from written sources in the period during and after the Exile. Basically the editor was working with three main sources, J, E, and P. In precisely what form those sources were when they came to him it is now extremely difficult to say. Moreover, there has been a great deal of discussion over the years about the dates of the original editions of the three, their purpose and their history. Generally speaking, it has been agreed that the J source is the oldest of the three, perhaps coming from the time of Solomon or even David, that the E source was produced about a century later, and that the P source comes out of the Exile. But in a sense all discussions of date are futile because it is also agreed that the three written sources have behind them long periods of oral tradition so that while the literary units in P may have only reached their final form at a relatively late date, nevertheless their original oral form may antedate the writing down of J and E.

In earlier days when the interest in these sources centered upon their historical value, the J source was much maligned. It was too obviously fanciful, too clearly composed of legend, saga, and myth, to be of any great interest to people whose primary concern was to ask historical questions. In this century, however, the attitude towards the J source has gradually changed. The forms of the stories that go to make up J's narrative have been carefully analyzed and studied. For the most part it is apparent that he borrowed his tales from the common store of folklore available to him amongst his own people. Some of the narratives that we have in Genesis he wrote himself, but most of them come from the oral tradition. And many of these oral narratives fall into the category of etiological legends, that is to say, they are stories that attempt to answer simple child-like questions, such as Why do people wear clothes? Why are there so many languages? or How did that well get its name? Most primitive peoples have etiological legends, and the Hebrews were no exception to the

11

rule.[1] It was these old tales, of little or no historical merit, that the J author skillfully wove into a theological masterpiece. And, with a few exceptions, it is his stories rather than those of E or of P that I have elected to retell.

The more one deals with these old narratives, the more one is impressed with the sophistication of their mode of presentation, with their arrangement, and with their content. But above all, if one takes the time to study them with care, and to live with them, one will find oneself entirely charmed by the insight of the unknown person who wove them together, and who placed an unmistakable stamp upon them. In spite of all the words that have been written about Abraham's faith, it is the faith of the J author to which these stories bear witness. It is his concept of God that they spell out. It is his understanding of humanity that they reflect. Back of Adam and Eve, Cain and Abel, Noah, Abraham, Sarai and Isaac, Jacob and Esau, Laban and Rachel and Leah, stands the J author, and to understand these stories, it is important never to forget that fact. Always the questions must be, What was J saying about where life's meaning is to be found? And it is these questions that I will be addressing to these stories in my comments. To be sure it is also true that back of the J author stands the community whose stories these also are, for it was the

---

[1]As a matter of fact, many families have their own etiological legends, for children between the ages of five and ten give parents many opportunities to evolve familial etiologies. I was, for example, a few years ago a participant in a study retreat at a United Methodist Church in Houston. Early in the course of that retreat, I went with certain members of the staff to eat a meal in a western restaurant. One of the staff brought his two younger children with him. After we had found ourselves a table, the waitress brought to the table a covered dish in which there were cornbread biscuits, which are popularly called "hushpuppies." When the bread dish had been passed around the table and it reached the children, they asked what was in the dish, and when they were told that the dish contained hushpuppies, they immediately asked why the cornbread was called a hushpuppy. The father, upon hearing the question, immediately told this story, variants of which I have frequently heard elsewhere in Texas: Once upon a time in this part of the world people were very poor. Many families had nothing but cornbread to eat for their meals. In the evening the mother would prepare the cornbread and the family would come in and sit around the table, and she would serve the cornbread to them. As they ate, the smell of the cornbread would go out the door to the dogs who would be huddled at the door; they, hungry too, would skulk into the kitchen, come closer and closer to the table, whining, begging for something to eat. The father would then take some of the cornbread and give it to the dogs and say, "Hush, puppy." And that is how cornbread cakes came to be called hushpuppies.

community that preserved them, shaped them, and poured its soul into them over the many centuries that preceded that first day when J wrote them down. And it was the same community that afterwards preserved them in their written form, cherished them, meditated upon them and discovered in them again and again the life that they still breathe. But in spite of the debt owed to the community, it was J who focused these stories for us and for them, perhaps according to a foreordained story form, and perhaps not.

It takes a courageous person to trust a message entirely to a story and not to explain it in full and gruesome detail. It takes a person with rare self-control. And yet that is the kind of person with whom we deal here. He tells his stories with very few comments. He even includes the old etiological elements. He permits his readers to do with them what they will, and many and strange have been the things they have done. But the option to the reader is open. If one wishes to be entertained, one may be entertained. If one wishes to laugh, one may laugh. If one wishes to hear, one may strive to hear. If one wishes to see, one may strive to see.

In the light of the old master's restraint, it is therefore both amusing and embarrassing to set about "to comment" on his stories. And yet, as I have indicated, the stories compel commentary. Nevertheless, in the spirit of the J author, I have tried to limit myself simply to a retelling of his old tales. Where I have succumbed to the lures of temptation, I hasten to excuse myself on the grounds that after all, the stories were written in a distant land, in a strange language, in a long forgotten day and therefore sometimes explanation is absolutely necessary. And secondly, since I have found these stories "a lamp unto my feet and a light unto my path," it is difficult to resist the desire to shout, "Look!"

There are many kinds of questions that one might address to these stories. One could ransack them for their historical allusions; or one could try to uncover the social and economic settings from which they came; or one could try to ascertain the religious milieu that produced them. Each of these areas provides a valid range of questions that can lead to profitable and interesting study. But my concern here is to remind the reader that whatever other matters may be of interest, one ought never to forget that the Church comes to us with the claim that these stories are indeed "Word of God"; that they in fact do tell us the very truth about God's nature, where we stand in relationship to him and something of what our common task is. Consequently, I would suggest that the reader always ask (1) what the stories say about the nature of God's attitude toward humanity; (2) what they say about the condition of human relationships with God and with one another; and (3) what hints they give about the way in which one ought to go. If one asks these questions honestly, and responds prayerfully, it will soon become much clearer why the Church has made such lofty claims for these simple old tales.

Finally, I need to say thank you to my parents for reading and telling these stories to me over and over again many long years ago, as their parents had previously done for them. Those memories have left a lasting impression. I need also to express my thanks to the students at Perkins School of Theology who have written papers on them for me, and have discussed them with me, and who have preached them to me. As the years pass I realize increasingly the extent to which I am their debtor. And then there are the laity in numbers of United Methodist and Episcopal churches throughout Texas and the Southwest who have participated in various kinds of groups with me, and especially the laity of St. Michael and All Angels Episcopal Church in Dallas, to all of whom I owe a debt of gratitude for their responses to these stories. And lastly to my wife, Waldine, who has listened to them over and over again, never failing to comment kindly and patiently, I give my heartfelt thanks.

—*W.J.A. Power*

PART I

Once Upon a Time

An Ideal Situation

One day, in the very beginning, when the world was nothing but a flat, empty plain, barren and unpopulated, the Lord God appeared upon the scene with a little potter's wheel under his arm. He set up the potter's wheel in the middle of the plain and prepared to go to work.[2] He had no trouble finding wet clay because every night a mist would go up from the ground to dampen it. So he took some and threw it on the spinning wheel. For a while he huddled over the wheel, working and fashioning. After a while he stopped, and took from the wheel a little clay man who looked for all the world like a gingerbread boy. Then the Lord God bent down and breathed a puff of breath into the quiet nostrils, and the clay man became a living bundle of appetites.[3]

The Lord God then planted a garden out in the plain, not just any garden, but a magic garden, into which he put the bundle of appetites that he had created. Out of the ground in that garden

---

[2]The Hebrew word that describes God's creative action here is *yasar*, which describes the creative activity of a potter.

[3]The Hebrew word is *nephesh*. This is a somewhat more colorful word than those English words by which it is frequently translated, e.g., "being", (NRSV; NJB; T; NIV; NAB), "soul" (KJV; Berkeley), or "creature" (REB; NEB). Like many Hebrew words that are rendered into English by abstractions, the word *nephesh* is a concretion. It describes humanity in terms of a concrete metaphor, "a gaping greedy throat" (Isaiah 5:14), "an appetite" (Isaiah 56:11), or a "craving or desire" (Psa. 35:25; Hosea 4:8). It speaks, in short, of humanity's appetitive nature, which we share with the animals (Rev. 24:18).

15

he made all kinds of trees grow, and in the middle of the garden he made two quite extraordinary trees grow—the tree of life and the tree of the knowledge of good and evil.[4]

The Lord God then took the man and put him in the garden in order that the man might till it and generally care for it. And the Lord God laid a command upon the man, "From every tree in the garden you may freely eat, but from the tree of the knowledge of good and evil you must not eat, for on the day that you eat of it you will die for sure." Then the Lord God stood back to survey the scene. And he came to an immediate conclusion.

He said, "It is not good for the man to be alone, so I must make him a companion."[5]

Then the Lord God went back to his potter's wheel and busily set to work. From the wheel that day there emerged a variety of animals and birds, which he brought to the man to see what the man would call them. And whatever the man's response to the animal was, that was its name.

If he said, "Skunk," it was a skunk. If he said, "Kangaroo," a kangaroo it was. If he said, "Armadillo," it was an armadillo. And soon the magic garden was full of the pleasant sounds of animals and birds, but for the man there was as yet no satisfactory companion.

Now the image changes. The potter's wheel is put away and when the Lord God next appears it is with a carpenter's toolkit in hand.[6] Then the Lord God caused a trance to fall upon the man.

---

[4]The Genesis narrative now proceeds to describe the location of the garden, although, as von Rad says, these verses must ". . . be considered as originally an independent element which was attracted to the story of Paradise but without being able to undergo complete inner assimilation." It says that there was in the vast plain a river that watered the garden. When the river left the garden it divided into four branches. We do not know the name of the first branch, but we do know the names of the other three. They are the Nile, the Tigris, and the Euphrates. The garden apparently is some place just beyond the point where these three known rivers and the mysterious unknown fourth separate from one another! The whole picture, of course, represents a cartographer's nightmare. It reflects the ancient misunderstanding of the nature of the relationship of the land mass to the ocean.

[5]The Hebrew word is 'ezer. It means a helper but it is usually used to describe God's relationship with humanity. Hence it does not mean an inferior, but rather one who enables a person to face a problem, or overcome a difficulty, or accomplish a task (Ex. 18:4; Ps. 33:20; 115:9, 10, 11).

[6]The Hebrew word is banah, which describes a builder, a master craftsman, a skilled artisan at work.

When the man had fallen asleep, the Lord God removed from his side one of his ribs, and with hammer and nails and plane he built a woman for the man. Then he woke the man and brought to him his new companion. As soon as the man saw the woman, he did what men have always done ever since, when they first see a woman. He burst into poetry, of course! "What a stroke of luck," he said, "I can see myself in you, so I'll call you woman."

And that's the reason why young men and young women leave their parents, and cling to one another, and become one even today.

★ ★ ★ ★ ★

Years ago I told this story of the magic garden to a group of children in a Sunday School class. When I was finished I asked them what they understood God to be like on the basis of the story. One precocious little fellow said, "That story says that God likes us." When I pressed him to discover why he had come to that conclusion, his response was that you would not go to that much trouble if you did not like the other person. My final question to him was, "What is it that the story says that a person needs?" To which he replied brightly, "Someone to love and with whom to be a friend."

This initial story in the Yahwist tradition portrays how things ought to be. It's a story about peace, not in the sense of absence of strife, but in the sense of relationships intact. Here is a portrait of an idyllic state: humans in harmony with one another through mutual respect; humans in harmony with God because they know they are under the divine command; and humans in harmony with the natural world around them because they know they have a responsibility to care for it and to love it.

Everyone's Situation

In the magic garden there was a very clever talking snake. One day the woman and the snake entered into a conversation. During the course of the conversation the snake said, ". . . and so God has said that you are not to eat from any tree in the garden?"

The woman, who now found herself in the highly desirable position of knowing what God has said and therefore of being able to put this know-it-all snake right where he belonged, answered in her most assertive fashion, "We may eat from the fruit of the trees of the garden. It is only concerning the fruit of the tree in the middle of the garden that God has said, 'You must not eat of it.'" And then she added words that were not in the divine command, "He said, 'you must not even touch it lest you die!'"

The serpent, however, was not to be outdone that easily. He said, "You won't die at all. God knows that on the very day you eat of it your eyes will be opened and you will become real, genuine gods, knowing everything that gods know."[7]

And with that he moved quickly off into the underbrush so that the woman was left alone.

The woman stood in front of the tree, eyes agog. She had information about it now that she had never had before. She realized that the tree was good for food, that it looked nice, and what was more important, that it possessed a unique gift of wisdom, so she took some of its fruit and ate it. Then she gave some to her husband, who was there with her, and he also ate it. With that their eyes were opened, and they realized something that they had not known before, *that they were unprotected, vulnerable, and in danger.* So they scurried off into the shrubbery, and set about making fig-leaf skirts in order to protect themselves.[8]

---

[7]See the translation in the TANAKH, ". . . you will be like divine beings who know good and bad."
[8]This in itself is a whimsical, humorous note, for most of us are allergic to fig-leaves!

In the late afternoon, when the evening breeze began to blow, the Lord God came down to take his customary walk in the garden. The man and the woman, however, were afraid of him so they hid themselves amongst the trees in the garden.

The Lord God, unable to find them, called out, "Where are you?"

The man replied from his place of shelter, "I heard the sound of you walking in the garden, but was afraid, because I have no protection. So I hid myself."

"Who told you that you were vulnerable?" came the divine reply. "Have you eaten from the fruit of the tree from which I commanded you not to eat?"

Then the man replied in words that make this story eternally contemporary, "If you had not given me her, I would not be in this fix. She gave me some of the fruit. What could I do but eat it?"

Then the Lord God said to the woman, "What in heaven's name have you done?"

The woman replied, "Well, sir, it was the snake who seduced me into eating it."

So the Lord God said to the snake, "Because you have caused this trouble, you are more cursed than all the animals; on your belly you shall go, and you shall eat dust forever. And you will never again carry on friendly conversations with humans; they will hate you and you will hate them. They will be continually on the hunt for you, and you for them."

To the woman he said, "I'll make you suffer for this! Whenever you scream in pain of childbirth, remember that you sought to be a god! You bossed your husband but from now on, he will be the boss!"

And to the man he said, "Because you listened to your wife's suggestion and forgot that I am your Lord, you will never again find life so easy. From this moment to the time when they lower you into the grave, sweat and thorns will be your wages for your work!"

By this time the fig-leaf skirts had begun to wilt, and the two humans appeared both pathetic and bedraggled. So the Lord God made them some decent skin tunics and dressed them up. And then, lest these two fear-ridden creatures should make the mistake of eating from the tree of life and thus wish upon themselves an eternity of anxiety, he mercifully banished them from the garden, and blocked the entrance with cherubim and a mysterious flashing sword.

And that's the way it is to this day.

★ ★ ★ ★ ★

Clearly the immediate death promised the man if he were to eat of the fruit of the tree was not biological. Both the man and his wife were very much alive. What was different about them was the feelings that they now had toward one another, toward God, toward the world around them. Fear is the word that the narrator uses of them. They were afraid of exposure and they hid because they sensed themselves to be vulnerable. So the narrator describes the human condition in terms of vulnerability, fear, isolation and estrangement. And this is also what he means by Death. The lonely, frightened, estranged human, although alive, is dead. As the text has already said with sublime understatement, "It's not good for man to be alone."

It is interesting to note that this state of lostness or death from which humans suffer is a feeling, a condition, grounded in an act, to be sure, but a feeling nonetheless. The act that leads to it is the refusal to accept the limitation, or one might say, the command that God has given. Be that as it may, what also emerges from this story is that God's feelings towards them *have not changed*. The changed feelings are on the side of mankind, not on God's side. He still comes looking for his lost creature, and the same words still echo today back of every fig tree in every fear-ridden garden. "Where are you?"

The First Thanksgiving Dinner[9]

After Adam and Eve had been expelled from the garden, they had two sons. The older of the two Eve called Cain, and the younger, she called Abel. Abel was a shepherd, while Cain owned a small vegetable farm. One year when the crops had been good, and the flocks had grown and expanded, the two brothers felt that they should give a gift to the Lord. They decided that they would hold a thanksgiving dinner at which the Lord, of course, would be present, for the Hebrews believed, as we do not, that the Lord was always present when people sat down to eat together. In this case, the Lord was to be the honored guest, the one for whom the meal was given. It was Abel's duty to bring the meat course, and it was Cain's duty to supply the vegetables. So Cain went to his stock and got some of this and some of that, and brought them for the meal.

Abel, on the other hand, went down to the sheepfold and picked out the very best lamb that he could find. He slaughtered it carefully, cut it up and brought the choicest cuts[10] for the meal. Then the two sat down to eat.

When the meal was over, the Lord said to Abel, "That was the best lamb that I have ever seen."

To Cain he said, "You didn't try very hard, did you?"

---

[9]The Hebrew text of this chapter has suffered in the course of its transmission in three places: (1) in verse 1 where it is not easy to understand precisely what Eve has said; (2) in verse 7 where the most of the Lord God's statement to Cain is obscure; and (3) in verse 8 where Cain's words to Abel have been omitted from the text.
[10]The fat pieces were considered to be the choicest cuts, and the Lord's portion (cf. Lev. 3:6ff).

21

Cain was disgusted and disappointed at the Lord's judgment. Although the Lord tried to remonstrate with him and, indeed, tried to encourage him to act differently, Cain was not encouraged. Instead, he decided that he would get his revenge. He invited Abel to go for a walk in the country, suddenly attacked him, and killed him.

Then the Lord appeared upon the scene and said to Cain, "Where is your brother Abel?" To which Cain replied, "I do not know. Am I my brother's keeper?"

Then the Lord said, "What in the world have you done?

Because you have heartlessly killed your brother, and spilled out his blood upon the ground, I am banishing you from human society and from the agricultural life of the settled community. You are to become a nomad, a vagrant, a vagabond!"

Cain, overwhelmed at his punishment,[11] replied, "But vagabonds are vulnerable to the whims of every group they meet. I"ll have no friends and no support. Any group that finds me can kill me!"

So the Lord put a mark on Cain to indicate to all that met him that Cain was under the Lord's protection. And Cain left the presence of the Lord to go out to wander in the land of wandering,[12] east of Eden.

Fear is not the only feeling that isolates us, nor is all of the fear that we experience to be condemned either as neurotic or unwarranted. We know very well, many of us, that we have good reason to be afraid, for we have it on the basis of the clearest and most unimpeachable evidence, to which vivid witness is given daily in the media, that we live in a jungle, inhabited by jealous, selfish, deceptive, murderous humans. We live east of Eden in a place where the question, "Where is your brother?" at best falls on deaf ears, and more usually falls on the ears of the uncomprehending. So we do well sometimes to be afraid. And Abel might well have profited from some fear. To give God one's best is a dangerous business. One who pursues such a course needs to have an eye fixed steadfastly on the goal, and at the same time to be well aware that what is ultimately pleasing to God is bound to provoke one's brother.

But there are other feelings that produce acts that lead finally either to estrangement or to what J calls living Death, and Cain serves well as an example. He brings his petty trifle to God to give thanks. One can almost hear him say,

---

[11]The Hebrew word is 'awoni. This is a very powerful word and it is difficult to indicate the intricacies of its meaning in English. It means not only "sin" but its consequences in terms of both "guilt" and "punishment."

[12]There is a play on words in the Hebrew text that needs emphasizing. In vs. 12 Yahweh says to Cain, "You will become ná' wánád in the earth." In vs. 14 Cain protests his punishment but uses the same words ná' wánád. In vs. 16 even though he finds himself under the merciful protection of the divine mark nevertheless off he goes to be a nad in the land of Nod, a place name that is derived from the Hebrew verb that means "To wander."

We give thee but thine own,
What e'er the gift may be,
All that we have is thine alone,
A gift, O Lord, from thee.

He does not understand that only the best will do, or if he understands, he is too selfish to give. When his brother's gift is accepted, he is consumed with jealousy, and although the two have just participated in a meal at which they have reaffirmed their mutual loyalties, Cain treacherously kills his brother.

It isn't only fear that isolates. Selfishness, hypocrisy, jealousy, and callous indifference destroy the fabric not only of our own lives, but also of the lives of those around us. And note where Cain ends—a wanderer in the land of Endless Wandering.

Regular Seasons[13]

As the years passed by human society was marked by increasing violence, and when the Lord saw that the wickedness of human beings was very great, and that they only thought about doing things that were evil, he was sorry that he had ever created them at all.

So he said, "I'm going to wipe off the earth every living creature that I have made—humans, animals, creeping things, and birds. I'm sorry that I ever made them."

There was one man, however, who had found favor with the Lord, and his name was Noah. In his case the Lord decided to make an exception. So the Lord gave him instructions to build himself a large boat. When he had completed the boat, the Lord told him that he was to enter it, along with all of his family, and that he was also to take along seven pairs of each kind of clean animal—a male and its mate, and a pair of unclean animals, a male with its mate. The same was also to be the case with birds. He was to take seven pairs of each kind of bird in order to preserve them alive on the earth. "Because," the Lord said to him, "in

---

[13]There are two flood stories which have been combined by the final editors of this narrative. The Yahwist flood story, which is retold here, is to be found in Gen. 6:5-8; 7:1-5, 7-10, 12, 16b, 17b, 22-23; 8:2b-3a, 6-12, 13b, 20-22. The other flood story, which is from the Priestly source, is to be found in Gen. 6:9-22; 7:6, 11, 13-16a, 17a, 18-21, 24; 8:1-2a, 3b-5, 13a, 14-19; 9:1-17.

seven days' time I am going to make it rain for forty days and forty nights on the earth, in order to blot off the face of the earth every living thing that I have made."

Without debate, although he must have had some questions, Noah faithfully followed the Lord's instructions in spite of their incredible nature, in spite of his advanced years, and no doubt to the merry tune of his neighbors' laughter! Within a week this aged man had built the boat, and had assembled all of the various kinds of animals. Then he put his family and the animals on board, and said farewell to his incredulous neighbors. Up the plank he went as they cheered him on, and he disappeared inside. Then a chilling thing occurred! The door to the boat suddenly began to swing, although there was no wind. It slammed shut. And those who were closest to it saw that the bolt on the outside moved slowly into place, although no human hand touched it!

There was a moment of hushed silence, and then the sky exploded! For forty days it rained, and the flood mounted on the earth, and the waters rose, so that the boat began to float, and places of refuge became increasingly scarce. Eventually everything that was on the face of the earth, everything that breathed, died. Every living thing was blotted off the face of the earth—humans and animals, reptiles and birds—everything, so that only Noah and his family and those creatures that were with him in the boat were preserved alive.

After forty days, the rain from the heavens stopped, and the waters began to decrease gradually from the face of the earth. Noah opened the window of the boat, and let out a raven which went flying back and forth over the surface of the water. Then, he let out a dove to see whether or not the water had yet subsided from the surface of the earth, but when the dove could find no place to land, it came back to him to the boat. After another seven days, he let out the dove again. And in the evening it came back to him with a freshly plucked olive leaf in its beak. So he knew that the water had now subsided from the earth.

After waiting another seven days, he released the dove again, but this time the dove did not come back to him. So Noah removed the covering of the boat, and found that the surface of the ground was drying. Then he built an altar to the Lord, and taking some of the clean animals and some of the birds, he offered them up as a burnt offering to the Lord. And when the Lord smelled the smell of the sacrifice, he said to himself, "I will never again curse the soil because of humans, though the bent of their minds may be evil from their youth, nor will I ever again destroy all life, as I have just done. As long as the earth endures, seed time and harvest, cold and heat, summer and winter, day and night, shall never cease."

Since George Smith's fortuitous discovery of the Gilgamesh epic in the archives of the British Museum in the 19th century, numerous accounts of the Babylonian flood story have come to light with remarkable resemblances to the biblical stories. Both the J story and the Babylonian tales seem to have derived from a common cultural heritage, but what is more pertinent here than their similarities is their dissimilarities, and of these the most striking is the fact that whereas the Babylonian stories are reflective of their polytheistic and pantheistic cultures, the flood story in J will have none of that. The Hebrew God is not a part of this world. On the contrary, He is its transcendent Lord and Judge.

At the same time, the note of grace freely given and, utterly unmerited, which is so characteristic of the J source, appears once more. We have noted it previously in the protective mark placed on the forehead of a frightened but guilty Cain. We have noted it also in the leather tunics with which the Deity replaced the pathetic, withering, fig-leaf skirts of a guilty Adam and a guilty Eve. In this story, grace comes to Noah, quite inexplicably and unexpectedly. He simply "finds favor" with Yahweh. We are not told why. All we know is that for God's own reasons a new possibility is offered to Noah, which he may take or reject. To take it means life. To reject it means death. Given his advanced years and the apparent absurd impossibility of the divine command, Noah's response is nothing short of fantastic. It would have been much more reasonable for him to have set Yahweh's demand to one side as outrageous. But Noah takes God's challenge seriously and lives.

There is both a bright side and a dark side to the story of Noah. On the one hand, it reiterates the theme that human society left to its own devices is dead and hell-bent on utter destruction. But on the other hand it indicates that faith, which, of course, includes obedience, leads to life.

There is an ultimate inevitability to the fate of Noah's contemporaries, but a note of hope is sounded if one is willing to run the risk of trusting a God whose commands seem so foolish.

That's the Way It's Been Ever Since

There was a time, long ago, when everyone on the face of the earth used only one language, with a limited vocabulary, so that it was easy for folks to understand one another. In those days, our ancestors migrated to southern Mesopotamia and settled down there. It was there they discovered how to make mud bricks, and how to build buildings, small and great. And having made that discovery, they said to themselves, "Come on, now. Let's build ourselves a city with a tower whose top shall reach into heaven, and that way we can make a name for ourselves, and we won't be scattered all over the earth."

So they started in to build their city with its tower, and when they had the city and the tower well underway, the Lord came down to get a better look at this magnificent construction at which the human beings were working. The Lord said, "Here they are, a single people, with a language that everyone understands. If this is what they are going to do with their unity, then what in the world will they end up doing? Come, let us go down and make such a babel of their language that they will never understand one another." So the next morning when the inhabitants of this new city awoke, everyone could talk but no one could understand anyone else. Because of the confusion and consequent misunderstandings, they had to stop building the city. Moreover, because of the fact that there is nothing that causes suspicion more quickly than a language barrier, their quest for unity was soon dissipated, and they began to scatter all over the earth.

And that's how the city, Babylon, (Babel) got its name.

Sermons on the futility of putting one's trust in the abundance of the things one possesses, or in the magnificence of one's mud brick towers, are at least as old as this story, for the key to it is to realize that to be nameless is to be non-existent, dead, as though one had never been. The rationale, therefore, for building the Tower is to gain existence—a rationale that is not without its relevance for our own day. So the dead seek to find life in the mud, in the dust from which they came and to which they shall return, but they find only confusion and more separation. In the mad quest for the life of abundance all communication breaks down, and each quester becomes an isolated, babbling unit, unheeding and unheard.

Thus the pre-patriarchal narrative come to their end after having stated the problem, that humans find themselves alone, and afraid, captives of their own guilt, victims of their own hubris, estranged from God, and cut off from their fellows.

PART II

Abram
An Average man

It is important to keep in mind while reading the Abram stories that he is not only the individual called into a relationship with the Lord, but also and more especially, that he is the elect group. Abram is *both* the called individual, *and* the called group. Indeed, if the emphasis is to be placed on either understanding, it ought to be placed on the latter. There is much, therefore, to be learned from these stories about the call of God's people, about the nature of the relationship established between God and his people, and about their purpose and function as his agents whether they be Jews or Christians. But what is even more important is what these narratives have to say about God's purpose in calling them, and about his determination to achieve his purpose in spite of their cowardice, stupidity, avarice, lust, generosity, kindness, devotion and faith.

The Call of an Average Man

Now there lived amongst this group of people, none of whom could understand the other, a man named Abram, whose plight was no better than that of any of his fellows. He also was one who could not communicate with anyone around him. But he was chosen by the Lord to be the father of that people through whom the Lord would work to resolve the dilemmas that faced humanity. He had a wife whose name was Sarai, who unfortunately could have no children, and in the light of the purpose for which Abram was chosen, that posed an added problem. And he had a nephew, his brother's son, whose name was Lot. It was therefore not on the basis of his obvious merits that the Lord chose Abram, and said to him, "Abram, leave your land, and your relatives, and your father's home, for a land that I will show you. I will make a great nation of you, and I will bless you, and I will give you the name that your forefathers sought when they set about to build the tower. It will be a name so great that it will be used for blessing. The security that they sought, the reputation and the life that they desired, you can have, if you will heed my call and come and follow me. Those who bless you, I will bless, and anyone who curses you, I will curse, and through you shall all the families of the earth be blessed." Like Noah, without question, without a word of response, Abram packed up his things, and set out to follow the Lord's command, and Lot and the barren Sarai went with him. After a long journey, he and his family arrived in the land of Canaan, where they built altars, and at one of those altars the Lord appeared to Abram and said, "This is the land. To your descendants I am going to give it."

★ ★ ★ ★ ★

The call of an average man contrasts nicely with the immediately preceding narrative. What the inhabitants of Babel sought in the mud, Abram is promised on condition that he trust and follow. Existence, genuine existence, life will be his reward, and all the families of the earth will share in his glory. On the face of it, the Lord should have called Abram does seem peculiar. The only way in which he stood out from the group was in his wife's incapacity to have children, and that made him a rather unlikely choice, all things considered. But throughout the Scripture the divine choice almost inevitably falls upon the least likely, upon those who are really incapable, in order that "no man may boast" when the task has been accomplished, and the goal achieved. Here the goal is to resolve the problems of the broken relationship with God, and to put together once again the shattered fragments of human society.

AN AVERAGE MAN IN ACTION
Part One

It was not long before Abram became disenchanted with the promised land. It is, of course, impossible to know exactly what it was that he anticipated before he came, but it is certainly clear that it did not long live up to his expectations. Shortly after he arrived there came a famine in the land, and in spite of the marvelous religious experience, and the ensuing long trip, Abram decided that Canaan was not for him. So off he went to live in Egypt, of all places. As he was about to enter Egypt, it suddenly dawned on him that Sarai was going to pose a considerable problem for him when he crossed the border. The trouble would come, he realized, because she was so attractive. So he said to Sarai, "Look, I know that you are a very beautiful woman, and when the Egyptians see you, they're going to say, 'This is his wife.' Then they'll kill me in order to get you. Please do me a favor when we get to Egypt: say that you are my sister.

31

Then I will be well treated because of you, and no one will kill me."

When they got into Egypt, sure enough, the Egyptians saw that the woman was very beautiful. And the word soon got around to Pharaoh. His courtiers praised her and told him how attractive she was, and so Sarai was taken into Pharaoh's harem. And because of her, Abram was given many sheep, and much cattle, and many he-asses, and even male and female slaves, and camels too. The Lord, however, saw that his plan for Abram could soon come to naught if Sarai remained in Pharaoh's harem, and therefore he struck Pharaoh and his household with severe diseases.

So Pharaoh, who somehow or other ascertained what the cause of the problem was, called in Abram and said to him, "What a way for you to treat me! Why didn't you tell me that she was your wife? Why did you say, 'She's my sister,' and let me marry her? Well, here's your wife. Take her, and beat it!"

Then, in order to make sure that Abram really did leave Egypt, Pharaoh sent an official escort after him to see him off with all that belonged to him.

★ ★ ★ ★ ★

Faced with his first hurdle, Abram snatched his future into his own hands and ran off. In order to protect himself from real or imagined danger he was forced into dissimulation, and straightway the promise was put into jeopardy. It was only the Lord's direct intervention that saved the situation.

This is one of those Old Testament readings that rarely appears in the lectionary or in Sunday School materials because the behavior of the patriarchal couple is so unacceptable. Here we have the picture of a man who is willing to sacrifice his wife to save his own neck. Can you imagine it? Of course, you can! What is even more remarkable is that she is willing to go along with him. Can you imagine that? And what is most remarkable is that God is with them to deliver them from the consequences of their duplicity for the sake of his own purpose. Can you imagine that?

AN AVERAGE MAN IN ACTION
Part Two

So Abram went up from Egypt to the land of Canaan, accompanied by his wife and all that belonged to him. Both he and Lot had profited from their Egyptian venture. Because of their extensive holdings in cattle and sheep, it was necessary for them to journey gradually from camping place to camping place until they came to the area between Bethel and Ai where Abram had previously erected an altar.

Now this area is not a particularly fertile area, and since they were both very wealthy with extensive holdings, the land was not able to support them both. Consequently trouble arose between their herdsmen. It might have got to the serious stage had not Abram one day said to Lot: "Look, we simply can't go on quarreling, nor can we permit our herdsmen to go on quarreling, for we are kinsmen. The whole land is open to you isn't it? You can take whatever you like. If you go to the left, then I'll go to the right. If you go to the right, then I'll go to the left."

So Lot looked out over all the land. He viewed the stony hills of the promised land of Canaan, and then he looked farther to the east and down into the Jordan valley, to the area around Sodom. There he noted the contrast, for the suburbs of Sodom and Gomorrah were well-watered, watered as well as the Garden of Eden, as well as the land of Egypt. So, Lot left the promised land, and went down into the valley, and chose it as his dwelling place. Thus he and Abram parted from one another.

Abram, then, was left with the hill country of Canaan, while Lot settled in the valley of the Jordan.

After Lot had left, the Lord appeared to Abram and said: "Look around, now, to the north, south, east and west, for all the land that you see I am going to give to you and your descendants forever. And I am going to make your descendants like the dust of the earth, so that it will be as possible to count the dust of the earth as to count your descendants. Go, travel the length and breadth of the land, for I am going to give it to you."

So Abram moved to the south and went to live beside the sacred oak of Mamre at Hebron, and there he built an altar to the Lord.

★ ★ ★ ★ ★

There is an element of tension in these two stories that is not always apparent to modern readers. In the first instance, because of his cowardice and duplicity, Abram put the promise and God's plan into jeopardy. If it had not been for the Lord, who know what might have happened in that oriental harem? As far as that goes, who know what did happen? In the second instance, Abram again put both promise and plan in jeopardy through his magnanimous generosity. This time it was Lot's avarice that saved him. In both instances the threat to the promises was real enough and in both instances the situation was saved not because of Abram but in spite of him.

Two Visions

One night the Lord appeared to Abram and promised him a vast reward. But Abram said to the Lord, "Oh, Lord, the only reward I really would appreciate is a child of my own."

So the Lord led him out of the tent, and pointed up at the stars in the cloudless sky, and said to Abram, "Can you count the stars? Thats how numerous your descendants will be." And Abram, with a barren wife, believed the Lord's word. Simple faith like that the Lord considered to be righteousness.[14]

On another occasion when the Lord told him that he planned to give him possession of the land of Canaan, Abram said to the Lord, "Lord, how am I going to know that I shall possess this land?"

So the Lord said to him, "Get a three-year-old heifer, a three-year-old she-goat, a three-year-old he-goat, a dove, and a young pigeon."

Abram got them, and cut the animals in two, but not the birds, and placed the pieces opposite one another as a sacrifice. And while he stood guard over the animals, down came birds of prey to devour their carcasses, but Abram drove them off. The afternoon light began to disappear, and as the sun was about to go down, suddenly, Abram fell into the same kind of religious stupor that Adam had experienced just before Eve was created.[15]

When the sun had set, and it was very dark, there appeared out of the sky a smoking fire-pot, and a blazing torch, which passed between the pieces of the animals. And that day the Lord covenanted with Abram, and said to him, "I am going to give your descendants this land, from the Euphrates to the border of Egypt."

★ ★ ★ ★ ★

In light of the circumstances, these two promises are incredible. Abram owned nothing and his wife could conceive

---

[14]15:1-6 have been a battleground for source critics. It is frequently assumed that the E source begins here. At the same time it is clear that there are doublets in the text from which, in my judgment, it would be precarious to try to isolate either the E or J sources. The abbreviated form of the story that I have told is therefore set out cautiously and without any inclination to cast my lot with a particular literary analysis of the verses.
[15]cf. Gen. 2:21.

nothing. But the promises are made anyway. And what is even more incredible is that Abram believed them. He believed God's absurd promises. That is a significant aspect of what faith is: to believe God's incredible promises about the future, namely that it is safely in his hands, both one's life and its significance. On the surface of it such promises are absurd. To believe that the God who revealed himself in Jesus is with us and will be "to the end of the age" is as incredible as the promises to Abram. And yet, righteousness is bound up in believing such absurd, unbelievable promises as these.

It is also noteworthy that God binds himself here, while all that Abram is called upon to do is to believe. One wonders whether in the last analysis even his "belief" is a necessary ingredient in the fulfillment of God's promises. Is it possible that God's grace could come to Abram, and like Abram to us, not because of his goodness, or his merit, or his believing, but simply because that is how God acts? Is it possible that even *our faith* is not a primary necessity for God's manifesting his grace to us?

How a Spring Got Its Name

The years were passing, and in spite of all of the Lord's promises to them, Abram and Sarai still did not have a son of their own. What little patience they had was slowly being frittered away, and finally, one day, Sarai said to Abram, "Look, the Lord is certainly not going to let me have any children. Why don't you just go to bed with my maid? Perhaps I might be able to build up a family through her."

Abram, for one reason or another, did not take much convincing. He went off to bed with Hagar, and in no time at all, Hagar had conceived. When she found that she was pregnant, and that, as a matter of fact, Abram's potency was not in question, but Sarai's capacity, Hagar treated Sarai with considerable disdain. Sarai, naturally enough, was irritated with her maid's haughtiness, and so she came to Abram and said to him, "Now look what you've done to me! May all of the wrong done me fall on your head! I let you sleep with her, and now that she's pregnant, she thinks she's better than I am! May God judge between you and me!"

Abram, however, was not prepared to intervene in the struggle between the two women. Very much like Pilate, he wanted simply to wash his hands of the whole mess. So he said to Sarai, "Look, she's your maid. You do whatever you like."

Sarai then treated Hagar so badly that Hagar ran away from her into the desert, where an angel from the Lord found her beside a spring. He said to her, "Hagar, where have you come from, and where are you going?"

She said, "I'm running away from Sarai."

Then the angel said to her, "The child that you are carrying is going to be a boy, and you must call his name Ishmael [God Heard], for the Lord has heard of your ill treatment. He will be a wild man. Everyone will be against him, and he will be against everyone else, and he'll live the nomad's life on the outskirts of his relatives."

So Hagar named the Lord who spoke to her El-Roi [A God Who Can be Seen], because, she said, "I saw God and I am still alive."

That's how the spring on the road to Shur came to be called Beer-Lahai-Roi [the spring where one saw God and still lived]. It's the spring between Kadesh and Bered.

★ ★ ★ ★ ★

The time between the moment of promise and the moment of fulfillment stretches on interminably, and not everyone possesses the patience or the wisdom "for the living of these days." To stand and wait is a much more difficult task than to act. Clearly Abram and Sarai were not up to it.

"What am I to do?" Is that not the question that we all ask? As though our doing really had some great and eternal significance, as though the establishment of his Kingdom really was contingent upon both our decisions and our actions. It is indeed difficult not to be able to see in all its detail what God proposes, and how he proposes to effect his plans, and yet that is precisely where we are always.

Is it not strange the kinds of persons with whom and through whom God chooses to work? What a pair they were, this weak, lusting male, and this haughty, vicious woman, who feel compelled to take the future into their own hands.

Hagar wasn't so terribly attractive either. In a sense—she got

37

what she deserved. Arrogance always does. But in another sense, she did not get what she deserved. Just a poor Egyptian girl, used, discarded, alone and pregnant, but not forgotten by the Lord.

In spite of Abram's sin the sequel shows that the Lord did not discard him. There was no manifest act of repentance, but God continued to come to him.

This is not to say, however, that sin does not bear its own fruit. God loved Abram, but Hagar remained pregnant. God loved Abram, but Hagar's descendants are with us today as living witnesses to Abram's impatience and to his lack of faith.

A Passing Stranger

One hot afternoon, Abraham was enjoying a siesta in the doorway of his tent, when he suddenly became aware of the fact that there were three men standing not far from him. As soon as he saw them, he roused himself, got up from the door of the tent, ran out to meet them, bowed himself to the ground in front of them, and said to them, "Sirs, do me the favor of paying me a short visit. Come and enjoy the shade of my tree. Let me bring some water in order to wash your feet, and let me prepare a small lunch for you that you may refresh yourselves. Afterward you can proceed on your journey."

They agreed to his proposal, and came into his camp. After they had stretched out under the tree, Abraham ran into the tent and said to Sarah, "Quick, Sarah, get some of the best flour that we've got and make some cakes for these fellows."

Then he ran off to the herd, and picked out a tender, plump bullock, and gave it to a servant to have it prepared. Then he brought them some yogurt, some cakes, and the bullock, and he set it all in front of them. After promising them little more than a lunch, he brought them a feast, and waited on them himself, as they sat under his tree.

For a while, the men ate in silence, and then one said, "Where's your wife, Sarah?"

She's in the tent there," he said.

The stranger said, "I'll be back in nine months' time, and at that time your wife Sarah will have a son."

Now Sarah was standing just inside the flap of the tent, listening to the conversation, and since she and her husband were very old, and since Sarah had passed through menopause, she was very much amused at what the stranger said. To herself she laughed and thought, "Here I am, an old woman, well worn-out, with a worn-out husband; who's talking about going to bed with him again?"

But the stranger said to Abraham, "Why is she laughing? Why is she saying to herself, 'Is it really possible for an old woman like me to have a child?' Is anything impossible for the Lord? I'll be back in nine months' time, and when I come back, she will have a son."

At that Sarah became afraid, not to say embarrassed, so she denied that she had laughed. "I didn't laugh," she said.

"Oh, yes, you did," he said.

And then the three men set out for Sodom and Abraham went along with them to send them on their way.

★ ★ ★ ★ ★

There are those who think that the incarnation is a uniquely New Testament image, but from this story one can see that the Lord appears incarnate in the Old Testament as well. He comes to Abraham here in the form of the passing stranger to whom Abraham shows his hospitality. And while they eat together the needy stranger reveals Himself to the patriarch as his incarnate Lord.

The story adds another element to the concept of faith, for faith means not only putting the future into God's hands, and leaving the meaning and significance of one's life to him, but it also means to serve him as He comes to us in the form of the Stranger.

At the same time this story also serves as a nice counter-balance to earlier Abraham narratives. Here Abraham stops thinking about himself. From a position of apparent strength he reaches out to those who apparently have no strength. He becomes the epitome of generosity and kindness, and in his generosity he receives not just Isaac but the presence of his incarnate Lord—a striking contrast to his earlier attempts at safeguarding his own interests, and pursuing the child of promise in his own way.

39

Intercessory Prayer

As Abraham and the Lord walked along the path toward Sodom, the Lord was thinking to himself, "Shall I hide what I am about to do from Abraham? He is going to become a great and powerful nation, and through him I intend that all the nations of the earth shall be blessed. No, I think I will tell him what I am going to do, in order that he may teach his children how to keep to my way by doing what is just and right."

So he said, "Abraham, the screams emanating from Sodom are very great, and the sin of Sodom is very grave. I feel that I must go down to see whether or not their conduct really does match the screams that are coming up to me. I want to know what the situation is."

When the Lord had finished this statement, the other two men who were with them bade them goodbye, and started off down the road to Sodom, while the Lord remained standing beside Abraham. After a bit Abraham turned to him, and said, "Lord, are you really going to destroy the whole city, both the good and the bad? Suppose in the city of Sodom there are fifty people who are good. Would you really destroy the whole place and not spare it for the sake of the fifty good people who are in it? Lord, do not do a thing like this, to cause the good to perish along with the bad, to treat the good and the bad alike. Should not the Judge of the whole earth act with justice?"

So the Lord said to Abraham, "Well, if I find in Sodom fifty good people, then I will spare the whole place for the sake of the fifty good ones."

But Abraham said to him, "Lord, I know I shouldn't be talking to you like this, for after all, I am merely your creation, but suppose that there be five short of the fifty in the city? Would you destroy the whole city because there were five less than fifty good people?"

"No, I will not destroy it," the Lord replied, "if I find forty-five good people in it."

Once more, Abraham said to him, "What if there were only forty there?"

"I will not destroy it for the sake of the forty," the Lord replied.

Then Abraham said to him, "Lord, don't be angry, but suppose there are only thirty there."

"I will not destroy it for the sake of thirty."

"What if there are only twenty?"

"I will not destroy it for the sake of the twenty."

And then Abraham said, "Lord, don't be angry if I ask you just one more question. Suppose there are only ten?"

"I will not destroy it for the sake of the ten," he said.

And as soon as he had finished talking to him, the Lord went his way and Abraham went home.

★ ★ ★ ★ ★

The Lord told Abraham what He was going to do in order that Abraham might learn a lesson from the situation and pass his learning on to his descendants that they might know the way of the Lord. What did He teach him? Is it not that the Lord's ear is finely tuned to the cries of those who are exploited, and that He is compelled by his awareness of their agony to act on their behalf? Note that no question is raised about the morality or the character of the sufferers. What draws his attention is their screams, not their innocence, their need, not their piety!

But there is a further and obscured implication to what is said that Abraham senses, and that is reflected in his later intercedings, which is that God comes not only to act on behalf of the sufferer, but also to judge those who cause the suffering. God's advent, in short, speaks not only of the One who is our Savior, but also of the One who is our Judge.

Trapped

When the two angels arrived at Sodom that evening, Lot was sitting in a prominent place in the gate of the city. When he saw them, he rose to greet them, and after paying the proper oriental homage, he said to them, "Sirs, come to your servant's house to spend the night, would you please, and let me provide water for your feet. In the morning you may go on your way."

But they said, "No, we will pass the night in the open."

But Lot begged them to come, and to spend the night with him, and eventually, they agreed. They went over to his house and there he had a feast prepared for them, and had special cakes made for them to eat, but before they could go to bed, the men of the city of Sodom, all of them, to the last person, surrounded the house and shouted to Lot, "Where are those fellows who came to your house tonight? Bring them out, that we may have intercourse with them!"

Then Lot went outside to talk to them, and closed the door behind him, and said, "Listen, friends, don't act in such a depraved way. These are men with whom I have eaten. They are now my responsibility. Here I have two daughters, two young girls. Take them, just don't touch these men who are my friends."

But they said, "Get out of the way!"

And another said, "This fellow comes in as a stranger and an immigrant, and now he's trying to pretend that he's a judge. You know, fellow, we'll treat you worse than them!"

Then they began shoving and pushing Lot, and trying to get to the door behind him to break it in, but in the turmoil and in the confusion, the strangers reached out and grabbed Lot, and pulled him into the house with them, and slammed the door.

Meanwhile, those who were closest to the entrance suddenly found themselves blind, groping about in darkness, and unable even to find the door! Inside, the men said to Lot, "Look, is there anyone else who belongs to you here in this city—sons-in-law, sons, daughters, anybody at all that belongs to you in this city? If there is, get them out of here, because we have come to destroy this place. The screams coming from it have reached God's own ears, so he has sent us to destroy it."

So Lot went out to get his sons-in-law who had married his daughters. He said to them, "We've got to leave this place at once."

They said, "Why?"

He said, "Because the Lord is going to destroy the city."

They thought that he was kidding, so they hooted.

When dawn came, Lot, who was quite confused and bewildered, still had not left the city. So the angels came to him, and they said, "Look, get out of here! Take your wife and the two daughters who are living with you, and get out of here, or you'll be swept away with the whole city!"

But he still hesitated, for after all, this was his city. But the men, because of the Lord's pity on Lot, took his hand, and grabbed his wife and his two daughters, and led them out forcibly, and left them outside the city, and then they said to them as they stood outside the city, "Look, Lot, leave this city. Run for your very life!

Don't even look back at it, for God's sake! Don't stop! Don't stop anywhere in the valley, just run for the hills as fast as you can, or you'll be dead if you stay here!"

But Lot said to them, "No, sirs, no! You've done me a great favor, I can see because you've saved my life. But I can't possibly run all the way to those hills. I'll die if I do that. Look, there's a little town over there. Let me run to it. It's a small one. Let me stay here. Isn't it a small one? Let me live there."

And the Lord said to Lot, "Look, I'll grant you this request. I won't touch that town. Just go there. I won't do anything until you reach it."

As the sun began to rise over the earth, Lot entered Zoar, and at that moment there came down from heaven sulphur and fire, which destroyed Sodom, and the valley area round about it, and all of the people who lived in the city, and all the vegetation in the land—everything was obliterated. But Lot's wife looked back, and she became a pillar of salt.

The next morning, when Abraham went to the place where he had stood talking to the Lord, he looked down into the valley, and all that he could see coming from what once was Sodom and its suburbs, was smoke, smoke rising from the valley as though it were a kiln.

★ ★ ★ ★ ★

In common parlance the sin of Sodom has to do with sexual aberration, but it is interesting to note that in the prophetic canon of the Old Testament Sodom's sin is perceived to be the exploitation of the defenseless. In Isaiah 1:10ff the prophet addresses the people and the rulers of the city of Jerusalem as "rulers of Sodom," and "people of Gomorrah." They try to substitute religious practices, liturgies, festivals, prayer and the like for fair play, the pursuit of justice, and the rights of the oppressed. In Ezekiel 16 the prophet indulges in a lengthy assault on Jerusalem whose sin he compares to those of Sodom in these words, "This was the sin of your sister Sodom: she and her daughters lived in pride, plenty and thoughtless ease, and did not help the poor and the wretched?" (Ezekiel 16:49).

Clearly Lot and his family were much attracted to Sodom's way of life. There are many who would have found it difficult not to be. It is also clear that they had a large stake in it. But fortunately for the family, Lot could still remember another time, and a better way, and was still motivated by the old desert custom of hospitality to the stranger. These obligations included not only food and shelter, but the responsibility to protect and care for those with whom one had eaten. Lot accepted those responsibilities, without any apparent possibility of reward, and in the face not only of personal ridicule, but also of tragic personal loss. Nonetheless, it was this devotion to the old ways that saved his life.

The True Origin of the Moabites and the Ammonites

Lot did not stay very long in Zoar. For reasons inexplicable, even to him, he found himself afraid to live there. And so, off he went, with his two daughters, to live in the hills, where they found a cave and settled down.

One day the older daughter said to the younger, "Our father is an old man, and nobody in this country is going to marry us, so let's get our father drunk, and then go to bed with him. Perhaps we can preserve our race through our father."

So that night, they made their father drunk, and the older one went to bed with him. He was quite unaware of what happened. Next morning the older said to the younger, "I went to bed with my father last night. "Let's get him drunk again tonight, and you go in and lie with him. Perhaps we can preserve our race through our father."

So that night they repeated the process. The younger one went in and stayed with the father all night. And again he did not know what had happened. Both of the girls became pregnant, and both bore sons. The older named her son Moab, and the younger named her son Ben-Ammi. These two bastards were the forefathers of the Moabites and the Ammonites.

★ ★ ★ ★ ★

Consider the case of poor Lot. There was a time when he was prepared to leave everything to follow in the way of his uncle Abraham. But avarice separated them. Lot chose the greener fields of Sodom over the stony pastures of the land of promise,

44

and found himself trapped in chaos and desolation. Ultimately we follow him to that lonely cave.

The images are slightly overdrawn, and perhaps too apocalyptic. But the point is clear: once you put your hand to the plow, do not turn back!

The Test of Genuine Worship

As the Lord had promised, Sarah and Abraham did have a son whom they called Isaac. There is not very much memorable said about Isaac. There are a few brief narratives recounted, describing incidents in his adult life, but the tale in which he plays the most dramatic role is not really a story about Isaac. It is a story about Abraham and the kind of worship that God desires.

One day God decided to put Abraham to the test. He said to him, "Abraham, I want you to take your son, Isaac, the one with whom you identify so closely, and go to the land of Moriah, to a place that I will show you, and there I want you to offer him up to me as a burnt-offering!"

What Abraham's response to this shocking request was the text does not record. It simply says that he got up early the next morning, assembled the materials for the sacrifice, and with his servants and Isaac in tow, set off for the land of Moriah. Three days later he saw the sanctuary in the distance, so he said to the servants, "You fellows stay here with the donkey while the boy and I go yonder to worship. We'll be back after a while." Then he loaded the wood for the sacrifice on Isaac, while he took in his own hands the fire and the knife, and the two of them set off together.

It was apparent to Isaac that something was missing, so he said to his father, "Dad, we've got the fire and the wood, but where's the sheep?" To which the old man replied, "God will provide his own sheep."

When they got to the designated sanctuary, Abraham built the altar, arranged the wood, tied up Isaac, and laid him out on the wood of the altar. But when he stretched out his hand to take the knife to kill his son, a voice from heaven cried out, "Abraham, Abraham! Don't touch the boy! Now I know that you really do worship me, because you have not withheld from me this boy with whom you identify so closely."

Then Abraham saw that there was a ram caught in a nearby thicket. So he took the ram and offered it up in place of Isaac who, one can safely assume, was happy to scramble off the altar and make his escape! And that is why they call that place Yahweh-yireh (The Lord will provide).

It is usually argued that this story comes from the E structure of narratives and I do not see any reason to disagree with that judgment. I have included it here because of its profound understanding of what genuine worship is. As Von Rad pointed out long ago, the test hinges on the father's willingness to give up Isaac and what that means. In fact Isaac signifies two things to Abraham: he is his hope for the future, and he is also the one who will give Abraham' life meaning and significance. So that day when God asked Abraham to give Isaac back to him, he was asking the old man to trust both his hope for future life and for a meaningful and significant existence to the Almighty. That's the test of genuine devotion to God.

A Faithful Servant and an Ideal Woman

The years passed, and as they passed, Isaac grew up. Eventually, his mother died and his father grew older. One day when Abraham was a very old man, he summoned the oldest servant in his household, the one who was in charge of everything that belonged to him, and made him swear on oath that he would not permit Isaac to marry a Canaanite girl, but that he would go to Abraham's own relatives and get a wife for Isaac.

The servant then said to Abraham, "Suppose that the woman whom I find is not willing to come back to this country? Should I take your son back to the land from which you came?"

Abraham responded, "You make sure that he does not go back there. It was the Lord who took me from my father's home in the land of my birth and who promised me that my descendants would inherit this land, and he will send his angel ahead of you to prepare your way, so that you will get a wife for my son there. But if the woman should be unwilling to follow you, then you are free from your oath to me. Only, never take my son back there."

So the servant swore his oath to Abraham. Then he took ten camels and set out on his journey, carrying with him all kinds of

gifts from Abraham, and eventually he came to the city where
Abraham's brother, Nahor, lived. It was at evening that he
arrived there, at the time when the women come out to draw
water from the well. So he drew near to the well and made his
camels kneel beside it. Then he prayed this prayer: "Oh, Lord,
God of my master Abraham, please be gracious to me today, and
be gracious to my master. I am going to take my stand here beside
the spring as the women come out to draw water. Let the girl to
whom I say, 'Would you please let down your pitcher for me to
drink,' and who says, 'Drink, and let me water your camels as
well,' let her be the one whom you have picked for your servant
Isaac. By this, then, I shall know for sure that you really are being
gracious to my master."

Before he had finished his prayer, out came Rebekah, the
granddaughter of Nahor, with a pitcher on her shoulder. She was
a very beautiful young girl. Down she came to the spring to fill her
pitcher, and as she approached the spring, the servant ran to her
and said, "Would you please let me drink a little water from your
pitcher?"

She said, "Drink." And she lowered the pitcher and gave him a
drink. When she had finished giving him a drink, she said, "I will
draw water for your camels too." So she emptied her pitcher into
the trough, and ran back to the well to bring more water. As she
filled the trough for the camels, the man looked at her, eager to
know whether or not the Lord had brought his mission to a successful issue.

As soon as the camels had finished drinking, the man took a
gold ring and gave it to her, and two gold bracelets, and then said,

"Tell me, whose daughter are you? Is there a place in your father's house for me to spend the night?"

"I am the daughter of Bethuel, the son of Milcah, Nahor's wife. We have plenty of both straw and fodder," she added, "and there's room for you to spend the night."

Then the man prayed again to the Lord, and said, "Thank you, Lord, God of my master Abraham. You have not failed to be gracious and true to my master. I know that I am on the right road, for the Lord has led me to the home of my master's kinsfolk."

The girl ran on ahead and told her mother what had happened at the spring. Now Rebekah had a brother whose name was Laban, who ran out to meet the man at the spring, when he saw the ring, and the bracelets on his sister's wrists, and when he heard what his sister had said. When he reached him, the man was still standing with his camels at the spring.

"Come on to our place," Laban said. "Why stand outside when we have a house ready, and a place for your camels?"

So Laban brought the man into the house, and he had the camels unharnessed, and he had them fed and looked after and watered, and then he looked after the men who were with Abraham's servant. Food and water were set before them, but before the servant ate, he said, "I cannot eat until I have told my story."

"Speak," Laban said.

So Abraham's servant said, "I am a servant of Abraham. The Lord has richly blessed him. He is a very great man. The Lord has given him flocks and herds and silver and gold and many slaves and many animals. Now, my master's wife, Sarah, after she was rather old, bore a son to my master, and to that son my master is going to leave everything that belongs to him. My master made me take this oath: he said, 'You must not marry my son to any daughter of the Canaanites, but you must go to my father's home, to my own relations, to get a wife for my son.' I said to my master, 'Suppose the woman will not follow me?' But he said to me, 'The Lord, in whose favor I have lived, will send his angel ahead of you, and he will bring your errand to a successful issue, so that you shall get a wife for my son from my own relations and my father's home. If they refuse you, then you shall be free from the oath to me.' So when I came to the spring I prayed to the Lord, and I said, 'If you would really bring success to this errand in which I am engaged, then permit that as I stand beside the spring the girl who comes to draw out water, and to whom I say, "Would you please give me a little water to drink out of your pitcher?" and who says to me, "You may have a drink, and I will also draw water for your camels," let that woman be the one whom the Lord has allotted to my master's son.' Before I could finish my prayers, out came Rebekah with her pitcher on her shoulder, and she went down to the spring to draw water. So I said to her, 'Would you give me a drink?' whereupon she quickly lowered her pitcher from her shoulder and said, "Take a drink, and let me water your camels too.' So I drank, and she watered the camels. Then I asked her whose daughter she was, and she told me that she was the daughter of Bethuel, Nahor's son. So I gave her a ring and bracelets, and I thanked the Lord, the God of my master Abraham who had led me on the right road to get the daughter of my master's relative for his son. Now then, tell me whether you are ready to treat my master kindly or not, so that I may go one way or the other."

Laban and Bethuel answered, "This is obviously the Lord's doing. We could hardly say no to you, or even yes. Here is Rebekah. Take her and go. Let her become the wife of your master's son, as the Lord has signified."

As soon as Abraham's servant heard these words, he thanked the Lord, and then he brought out articles of silver and gold and clothing, which he gave to Rebekah, and he also gave gifts to her brother and mother, and then he and the men who were with him had something to eat and drink. With that they retired for the night.

The next morning, the servant said, "Now we must go to my master."

But the family said, "Let the girl stay with us a little while longer, at least ten days, and then let her go."

"No," the servant said, "don't stand in my way now. For the Lord has brought my errand to a successful issue and I must go back to my master.

"Well, we'll call her in and ask her what she wants to do," they said. So they called in Rebekah, and said to her, "Would you go with this man?"

And she said, "Yes."

So they let their sister Rebekah go with her nurse and Abraham's servant, and they bade her goodbye with blessings.

Rebekah then started out with her maids riding on the camels, following Abraham's man. Now, Isaac had moved from the neighborhood of Beer-Lahai-Roi, and was living in the land of the Negev. One evening as he went out for a stroll in the fields, he saw camels coming in the distance. Rebekah also at that moment lifted her eyes and saw Isaac, and she dismounted from her camel and said to the servant, "Who is the man yonder who is walking through the field toward us?"

"He is my master," the servant said.

So she took her veil and covered her face.

When the servant had told Isaac all that he had done, Isaac brought her into his tent and married Rebekah, and she became his wife. In loving her, Isaac found consolation for the death of his mother.

★ ★ ★ ★ ★

Whatever else one may want to say about Rebekah in terms of her relationship with her two sons, there is a golden moment in her story when she is used to exemplify what a Hebrew woman ought to be. She is kind and generous to strangers, and she is eager to fulfill the Lord's will. So be it!

As for the servant, the Old Testament also lays great stress on the importance of keeping one's vows, and assures us repeatedly that angels guard those who are devoted to their duty and strive to fulfill their promises.

★ ★ ★ ★ ★

With this charming tale of the servant's successful quest for a wife for Isaac, the stories about our father Abraham come to an end. What does one say about him? The apostle Paul repeatedly refers to Abraham and uses him as the example of the man of faith. One cannot deny that Abraham has his moments of heroic faith. One can only stand in awe of his willingness at his age to leave behind the traditional security symbols and to set out for an unknown land with a barren woman to become the father of a great nation. Moreover, his readiness to share his wealth with Lot, and with the wandering strangers later, is exemplary. But Abraham and Sarah were not paragons. They were quite capable of unfaith and of its concomitants fear, selfishness and cruelty.

If one picks and chooses, one can make Abraham into a model figure, but the J writer does not do that. He leaves us with a complete picture of Abraham, including his weakness, for when all is said and done, this story is not the story of a man's heroic accomplishments. It is, on the contrary, the story of God's patience, his persistent leading, his undying love, and of his determination to work through the descendants of Abraham that all the families of the earth might be blessed.

PART III

God's Chosen People
A Caricature

The story of Jacob is the story of Israel. It is a self-portrait. Perhaps it is slightly distorted, but if so the purpose of the distortion is to draw attention to the more glaring defects in Israel's character in the hope that the reader might reflect and then reform. And yet one ought not here to be looking for lessons on how to live. As is the case with most satires, one is not given specific advice; one is simply invited to see oneself as others do.

This is the story of God's dealing with and through an unscrupulous group of people who in microcosm are all of humanity. They are obviously self-centered, hypocritical, quick-witted, and deceptive rogues. Moreover their deception, hypocrisy and avarice leave behind a trail of broken relationships and sorrow, and they themselves reap their own harvest of loneliness, fear and grief. Nevertheless, it is not a gloomy story. It is filled with a hope based not on Jacob's treacherous skullduggery but on the grace of Israel's God.

Hairy and Grabby

Once upon a time there was an old man and an old woman who had had no children. Like many old men and old women who have found themselves in this situation, the two prayed to the Lord that they might have a baby. And the Lord yielded to their entreaties. The old woman conceived.

Soon she discovered that she was not only pregnant, but doubly pregnant, that she was carrying twins. The only grief in this otherwise happy state was that it quickly became apparent to her that the two were not going to get along well, for they had hardly been conceived before they began to carry on a regular wrestling match *in utero*. Faced with these distressing circumstances the unfortunate woman went to the local oracle in the area where they were living in order to ascertain from it what was to be done.[16]

The oracle, in typically oracular fashion, answered her cryptically: "Two nations are in your womb. The two have been hostile ever since conception in you. The one shall master the other, and the older shall serve the younger."

In due course the day came for the two to be born. The first child was born red and covered with hair, so they called him "Hairy." The second was born holding on to his brother's heel, and so they called him "Grabby."

★ ★ ★ ★ ★

Because of its puns, this story demands some comment. Esau was born red, *'admoni*, an obvious play on Edom, and he was born hairy, *se'ar*, a pun on Seir, an area of Edom where Esau was later to live. Both his reddish complexion and his hairy body speak to his lack of sophistication, a characteristic that the later narrative will continue to emphasize. Jacob was born grasping his brothers heel, *'aqeb*, a pun on his name. There is also a related verb on which there is a possibly play here, *'aqab*, which Holladay defines as "to grasp by the heel," or "to cheat." This verb appears in the narratives in 27:36, clearly referring to Jacob was the colloquial heel, ready to shortchange on each and every occasion, grasping and claiming for himself whatever he could get, and to the end holding on (cf. 32:27). But one must not forget that this scheming, conflicted grasper is God's chosen people. Naturally, those who are outsiders, like Esau and the Edomites, are always uncivilized, and just a little "hairy" to those who are on the inside.

---

[16] The Hebrew text is uncertain. *The Complete Bible: An American Translation* reads, "If it is to be thus, on whose side am I to be?" This is a question many parents ask daily.

In the course of time, the boys grew up. Hairy became a skillful hunter, doing a man's job, and living in a man's world. As a consequence, he became his father's favorite, for his father liked the wild game that he caught, and the way that he cooked it on an open fire. Grabby, on the other hand, stayed at home and learned to do the tasks that women do in the tent, and as a consequence, he became his mother's favorite. So the sibling rivalry that was born in the womb was further exacerbated by parental favoritism.

One day Hairy came in from the field starving, and found his brother Grabby working over a hot stove with a great pot of soup. Hairy said to his brother, "Give me a swallow of that stuff you're cooking. I'm starving." How will God's chosen people respond to the hungry brother's request? Well, the response and its consequences are dramatically different from those of his forefather Abraham, and for that matter, his great-uncle, Lot. They would have responded more generously.

"I'll be glad to give you some of my soup," said Grabby, "if you'll pay for it."

"I'll pay for it," said Hairy, "What do you want?"

"Let me have your share of the inheritance, and you can have some of my soup," said Grabby.

That gave Hairy something to think about. But present self-gratification was more important to him than the future.

So Hairy said, "I may die if I do not get something to eat, and then obviously my inheritance will have no value to me, so you can have it."

"Well, then, if I can have it, swear to me," said Grabby. "Give me your oath."

So Hairy gave him his oath, and Grabby gave him a dish of lentil soup, and Hairy ate the soup, got up and walked off.

This is a story about a sense of values, but it also illustrates why the one is called Grabby and the other Hairy.

The Charade

As time passed, the boys' father, Isaac, grew blind and eventually took himself off to bed on the assumption that he was soon going to die, although as a matter of fact, many years were to slip by before death took him and "the secret of his life" (von

Rad) with him to the grave. The father, for good or ill, had opted out, and the mother, was about to fill the vacuum.

One day Isaac called in his older son, Hairy, and said to him, "Son, I may very well die any day now. Do me a last favor. Take your bow and arrow, and go out into the fields, and get the kind of game you know I enjoy. Prepare it the way I like best, and bring it to me to eat. After I've eaten, I'll give you the power of my blessing."

Now, the boys' mother Rebekah, was listening to the conversation, so she heard what Isaac said to Hairy. As soon as Hairy had gone off into the field to do his hunting, she summoned her favorite, Grabby, and said to him, "Grabby, I just heard your father say to Hairy, 'Go and get me some of the game that I like best. Prepare me the kind of dish I like to eat, and I will give you my blessing before I die.' Now then, son, you do what I tell you to do. You go to the flock and get two fat kids for me. I will make them into the kind of tasty dish that your father likes best. Then you can take it to him, and he'll give you the blessing instead of your brother."

Grabby now found himself in an extremely difficult position. Everyone knew how an old, blind father ought to be treated. And most particularly, everybody knew how God's chosen people ought to honor their fathers. At the same time, however, everyone knows the kinds of pressure that mothers can exert upon their sons. What was Grabby to say? Of course, he couldn't say to his mother, "I've just seen an advance copy of the Ten Commandments and they require one to honor both of one's parents." What was he to do? Was he to encourage her to live a better life, and to adopt a more responsible attitude toward her

husband? Well, Grabby did what many of us do when caught in similar situations.

He said to his mother, "Mother, you didn't call him Hairy for nothing! Suppose my father were to touch me? He would discover that I am an imposter, and then I would get quite the opposite of a blessing. What would happen to me?"

In spite of the fact that in the ancient world the curse of a dying patriarch was customarily taken with the utmost seriousness, his mother replied, "Don't worry, son, I'll take the full responsibility for what happens. Let any curse for you fall on me! You just do what I tell you to do. Go to the sheepfold and get the kids."

So Grabby, now relieved of the threat of his father's curse, and with nothing whatsoever to lose and a good deal to gain, went off to the sheepfold and brought back the kids to his mother. She dressed them, and prepared them in the manner that the father liked best. She raided Hairy's closet, and dressed Grabby in Hairy's clothes so that he would smell right. Then she took the skins of the kids and put some of them on his arms and some on the back of his neck, and then, having prepared the food, she ushered the young man into the father's presence. Now it was up to Grabby to demonstrate how well he could lie and deceive.

"Dad?"

"Yes," replied the old blind man, "Who are you, my son?"

Without any hesitation, he lied, "I am Hairy, your first-born. I have done what you told me to do. Sit up, and eat some of my game, and give me your blessing."

But the father had been around God's chosen people long enough to be suspicious, so he said to his son, "How in the world did you ever come to find it so quickly?"

Once again he lied, "Because the Lord *your* God brought it into my path."

Then the father said to Grabby, "Come up a little closer. I want to touch you. I want to see whether you really are my son Hairy or not."

So Grabby went up to his father, who touched him and said, "Well, you sound like Grabby, but you feel like Hairy." And so he did not detect him.

Then the father made an appeal to the boy's conscience. "Are you really my son Hairy?" he asked.

"Yes, sir," the boy replied.

So the father said, "Well, then, bring me some of your game to eat, and I will give you my blessing."

So Grabby brought the game to him, and the father ate it. And he brought him some wine, and the father drank it.

Then the father said to him, "Come up here and kiss me, my son." So Grabby approached his father, who kissed him, and while he was kissing him, he tried his best to get a good smell of him! Then, having had recourse to all of the tests open to a blind man, the old fellow gave Grabby his blessing.

When the blessing was complete, and Grabby had left the room, in from the field came Hairy with his preparations for the father's meal. He went to work, prepared the kind of dish the father liked, and brought it in to him.

"Sit up, Dad," he said, "and eat some of your son's game and give me your blessing."

"Who are you?" his father asked him.

"I am your son," he said, "your first-born son, Hairy,"

And now we get a glimpse into the hell that selfishness and deception can create. The father, old and blind, sat up in his bed, greatly agitated.

"Who is it who got me some game and brought it to me? I ate of it before you came in, and I gave him my blessing, and so he has it," he groaned.

Hairy, upon hearing his father's words, cried loudly and bitterly, "Can't you give me a blessing too, Father?"

But the father replied, "Your brother came under false pretenses, and he stole your blessing."

"Is it because his name is Grabby that he has twice now grabbed things from me? He grabbed my birthright. Now he has grabbed my blessing. Haven't you got a blessing for me?" he begged.

But Isaac could only say to his son, "I've given him everything. What in the world can I give you?"

"Give me some little blessing. Give me some little blessing."

And in the midst of the tears which poured down Hairy's face, the father gave him a blessing, a blessing that in fact was only a curse.

So Hairy went about muttering to himself, "If I ever get my hands on him, I'll kill him."

And the mother, who always seemed to be aware of other

people's conversations, learned what Hairy had to say. So she sent for her younger son Grabby, and she said to him, "Grabby, I understand that Hairy is threatening to kill you. So, son, do what I tell you. Go north to my brother Laban, and stay for a little while with him, just a few days! Then your brother's anger will subside. You know what he's like. And when he has forgotten what you've done to him, I'll send and bring you back from there."

So Grabby obliged his mother again, and left for his uncle's home. He was to be gone for just a little while, but days passed into months and years. Eventually he did come home again, but by that time his mother who had schemed for him was dead and buried. The father, of course, was still in bed, but that is another story unfortunately omitted from the canon.

What Kind of a God Is This?

One night in the course of his journey, Grabby settled down to sleep at a local sanctuary without apparently realizing where he was. And during the night the Hebrew God appeared to him. What the Deity said to Jacob is bound to be a surprise to those who see the God of the Old Testament as a God of wrath or as punishingly vindictive. There is here a warm note of grace for those who have ears to hear, but Jacob, as it turned out, did not fall into that category.

God said to him, "Grabby, I am the God of your fathers, Abraham and Isaac. The land on which you are lying I intend to give to you and to your descendants after you, who will become as numerous as the dust on the ground, and who will spread all over the world, so that all nations on the face of the earth will be blessed because of you and your descendants. *Wherever you go I will go with you; I will protect you; and I will bring you back again to this land. I will never forsake you until I accomplish my purpose.*

In the light of what had just happened, and most particularly in the light of all the deceitful and dishonorable things that Grabby had just done, these were most remarkable promises. Nevertheless, Grabby's response to God's manifested grace was the bored response of many people who have become tired of the good news of God's love for them. He said, "Ho-hum. The Lord must have been here and I did not even realize it."[17]

It Takes One to Know One

For days Grabby plodded on towards the north. And then one day, he found himself beside a well in an open field. Around the well were three flocks of sheep with their shepherds. The stone that covered the well was still in place because it was far too large for one or two or even three shepherds to remove it, and in any case, they had all agreed that no one or two of them would ever remove it without all those who shared the right to the water being present.

"Where are you from?" Grabby asked the shepherds.

"We come from Haran," they answered.

"Do you know Laban, the son of Nahor?" he asked.

"We do," they acknowledged.

"How is he?" he asked.

"He's fine," they said. "Here comes his daughter Rachel now with his sheep."

Grabby said, "Why don't you get to work? What's the reason for your killing time here beside the well?"

They replied, "We are not supposed to remove the stone from the well until all those who participate in the water rights are present. So we can do nothing!"

While he talked to them, Rachel, the daughter of his uncle Laban, arrived. As soon as he got a look at her, and in spite of their carefully stated scrupulosity about water rights, he ran up to

---

[17]There is a second tradition here (E?), which also describes Jacob's response. It says, that in the morning when Jacob awoke, he took the stone that he had been using as a pillow, set it up as a sacred pillar, poured oil on it, and said, "Now Lord, if you really will go with me, and protect me on this journey that I am taking, and if you will give me food to eat and clothes to wear and if you will bring me home safely, I'll tell you what I'll do for you: I'll worship you, and I'll give you ten per cent of everything that you give me!"

It is difficult for some of us to believe that God graciously and freely loves us. We prefer to bargain. We prefer a *quid pro quo* agreement. So did Jacob. Moreover, by comparison with most of us, Jacob's offer is rather generous. Nevertheless it is met only with silence, for the prerequisite for God's grace is not human merit, no matter how great, nor human bargains, no matter how generous. The prerequisite for God's grace is need. And Jacob, whether he realized it or not, was a very needy person indeed.

the well, and with super-human strength took the stone and hurled it from the well, and busily watered the flock of his uncle Laban. Then he ran up to Rachel and kissed her. The text does not say what motivated him. Although one could probably guess, it is helpful to know that Rachel was a marriageable cousin, for it was the custom in those days, and in some parts of the Arab world it still is today, for boys to marry their mother's brother's daughters. He told her who he was, and she ran off home to tell her father. As soon as Laban heard that Grabby, his sister's son, had come, he ran out to meet him, and welcomed him into his house. That night, as they all sat around the fire, Grabby told Laban his whole story, and at the end of it, Laban muttered words of ominous import.

"You really are my own flesh and blood," he said. So Grabby settled in to live with Laban.

Like Brother, Like Sister

When Grabby had been living with Laban for a month, his uncle one day entered into a discussion with him about wages.

"Just because you're a relative of mine you can't work for me for nothing," he said. "What would you like me to pay you?"

Now Laban had two daughters. The older of the two was named Leah, and the younger was named Rachel. Rachel was a shapely attractive young woman but something was wrong with Leah's eyes. They lacked fire, dash, life. Perhaps she didn't know how to use her eye makeup well. No matter, Grabby has fallen in love with Rachel and will have her. So he made Laban a generous offer, "I'll work seven years for you for Rachel, your younger daughter." Laban's careful response was, "Well, it would be better for me to give her to you than to anyone else, so stay with me."

For seven years Grabby worked for Rachel, and the years seemed like only a few days because he loved her so much. When the time was up, he came to Laban and said, "Give me my wife. The time us up. I want to marry her."

Now, the custom in that part of the world was for the father to gather all of the men of the area together to hold a feast to celebrate the coming marriage. When all the men were gathered together, the party began, and in the evening the veiled woman was ushered into the marriage tent that Grabby might take to himself his bride. What with the darkness, her silence, and his excitement, it was not until dawn that he discovered that he had the wrong woman! Out of the tent he stormed, and made straight for Laban, to whom he said, "What a way for you to treat me! Didn't I work with you for Rachel? Why did you cheat me?"

Laban's laconic response was, "Well, in our country, it isn't customary to marry the younger daughter before the older." One would have thought that Laban might have mentioned this to Grabby sometime during the preceding seven years, but apparently it had slipped his mind!

So he said to Grabby, "You finish the week's festivities, the partying for this one, and then I'll give you the other one in return for another seven years' service."

Grabby agreed. What else could he do? The shrewd bargainer had been outwitted! So he finished the first week's activities, and then Laban gave him Rachel in marriage. Needless to say, Grabby loved Rachel, and loved her much more than he did Leah, who was shunned and treated rather badly. But the Lord, in whose heart there is a special place for all those who are ignored and unloved, looked after Leah, not because of her merits, but because of her need. So Leah became pregnant, and the mother of many children, while Rachel, the well-loved, was for a long time barren.

Getting Even

Many years had passed. Leah had borne Grabby many children, and Rachel had borne him one. Their handmaids also had borne him many children.

So one day, Grabby went to Laban, his father-in-law and uncle, and said to him, "Let me go. I want to go back now to my own country. I want to take my wives and my children with me. It's time for me to go."

Laban said, "How much would you like me to pay you for all the work that you've done for me?"

Grabby replied. "I don't really want any wage from you."

"What can I give you?" Laban asked.

"Oh, nothing," Grabby said. "I have worked hard for you—you know how hard I've worked for you. You know how you've prospered with my help. You know how numerous your flocks are now, but I need nothing."

"Oh, let me give you some kind of a wage," Laban persisted.

So Grabby said to him, "Well, if you insist. Here is the wage that I'll take: I'll take all of the culls from your sheep and goats, all those sheep that are not pure white and all those goats that are not pure black, the sheep that have spots on them and the goats that have spots on them. I'll take them, and you take just the best."

Now, Laban could hardly argue with such an arrangement, so he agreed that that would be Grabby's pay. Then Grabby, in order to insure that his father-in-law would not suspect him of any duplicity, said to him, "Separate the culls from the pure white sheep and the pure black goats and have your sons look after them, so that you can be sure that the culls do not ever get back amongst the pure white sheep and the pure black goats. And I'll look after only the best ones." And Laban agreed.

In order to understand what happened at this point in the story, it is important to realize that the shepherds believed that if you could catch the sheep and goats while they were breeding, and wig-wag the equivalent of checkered flags in front of their eyes, that the little kids and the little lambs would be born black and white, or checkered, or spotted. And so, for the next few months, you must imagine Grabby's scurrying about in front of the water troughs, wherever the sheep and goats were breeding, wig-wagging his checkered flags. Then, in the course of time, when Laban came to see his cherished flocks, all the sheep and all the goats were covered with black and white spots!

It was at that time that Grabby began to feel a strong urge to return to the land of Canaan, for he noticed that Laban's attitude toward him was not what it had been!

Farewell To Laban[18]

One day while his uncle was off doing some work in a distant field, Grabby put his belongings together, and took his wives, his

---

[18]The text as it stands has been much amplified by the E(?) tradition where the main emphasis seems to be placed on the incapacity of the household gods to be of

children, and his extensive flocks, and set out for home. When Laban learned of his departure, he pursued him, and since, of course, Laban was traveling light in comparison with Grabby, he readily overtook him.

"Why did you run off in secret without telling me that you were going? And why did you robe me?" Laban asked. "I'd have been glad to have sent you off with the biggest party you ever saw, with all kinds of hilarity and songs and music."

"I was afraid," Grabby replied. "I thought that maybe you would take your daughters from me by force, and so I ran off."

Then Grabby grew angry with Laban, and self-righteously reminded Laban of all the things that he had done for him over the previous twenty years, how he had looked after Laban's sheep and goats, and how he had borne the responsibility for all the lost animals himself, and eventually, at the end of his long tirade, he and Laban agreed to make a covenant between them, to which the Lord would be the witness. They set up a cairn of stones, and ate a meal beside the cairn, and declared that the cairn was to be a witness over them that day, that Laban would never come south of the cairn, and that Grabby would never go north of it, and that the God of Abraham and the God of Nahor would be judge between them.[19]

And so they agreed, and Grabby left Laban to head south.

Trapped

It was only when Laban had disappeared from sight that Grabby began to realize that not all of his problems were behind him. The last word that he had received about his brother Hairy was the word that his mother had conveyed to him that day so long ago, that Hairy wanted to kill him. And now Grabby realized that Hairy and the problem of the deception of Hairy lay in front of him.

So he decided that he would soften up his brother. He sent messengers ahead of him with an obsequious message for Hairy.

---

any real use to Laban. His frantic search for them, and his failure to find them further signified the folly of worshipping such nonentities.

[19]Some editor has added to the text a not inappropriate blessing. He has put into the mouth of Laban these words: "May the Lord protect us from one another when we are out of one another's sight!"

He said, "Thus you are to speak to my lord Hairy. Thus says your slave Grabby, 'I have been living these past twenty years with our uncle Laban, and I have become rather wealthy in the course of that time. So I am sending this brief message to my lord in the hope of finding favor with him.'"

The messengers rode off with the message, but shortly they returned to Grabby and gave him this distressing news, "Here comes Hairy with four hundred men!"

You can very well imagine how terrified and distressed Grabby was! What was he to do now? His flattery apparently had not appeased his brother who obviously had not forgotten the trick that had been pulled on him so long ago. Laban was behind him; Hairy was in front of him. There really was nothing left for him to do but pray!

So he knelt and said, "Oh Lord, you yourself have acknowledged that you were the God of my father and of my grandfather. You yourself were the one who said to me, without any prompting on my part, that I was to go home, and that you would look after me. I also recall that you were the one who revealed yourself to me many years ago, and made me some promises that I did not extort from you. Now I know that I have certainly not deserved all of the various things that you have done for me over the years—how you have cared for me while I was dealing with that rascal Laban—but Lord, all of your past deeds and past promises really don't have very much value unless you can now save me from my brother Hairy. I know, I really do know, that he is going to come and kill me, and perhaps he will even kill my wives and children. And Lord, if he kills me, and wipes out my children, then how in the world will your promise ever be effected? Amen."

There was no answer from heaven.

The Stranger

What was Grabby to do now? Flattery, obviously, was not going to work. Prayer, in this instance, had not changed a thing. What was he going to do?

That night he took his two wives and their two female slaves and his eleven children, and he sent the women and the children across the river Jabbok, which had separated him and his family from Hairy, and he sent across with them everything that belonged to him, and he stayed alone in the camp. While he sat there all by himself, accompanied only by his fears and his thoughts, a stranger appeared in the camp. Was this stranger God's answer to his prayer? If so, Grabby missed his opportunity, for he did not ask the stranger his name, nor did he offer the stranger the benefit of a meal, nor did he invite him in to share the comfort of his camp. He simply attacked him, and the two fought until the day began to dawn. And when the stranger discovered that he could not master Grabby, he touched the socket of his thigh so that his thigh was dislocated as he wrestled with him.

And the stranger said to Grabby, "Let me go. The dawn has come."

But Grabby replied, "I will not let you go unless you give me a blessing."

The stranger said to him, "Tell me your name" (which is the equivalent of saying, "Tell me who you really are," to which he replied, "I really am Grabby."

Then the stranger said to him, "You think that your fighting has only been with men. You think that you have stolen only from men. But in stealing from those around you, you have stolen also from God. In fighting with those around you, you have been fighting with God. And so I will call you not Grabby, but Israel, that is to say, the One Who Fights With God."

"Who are you?" Grabby asked.

"Why do you want to know my name?" the stranger replied. And then he left.

So Grabby called that place Peniel (the face of God) because, he said, "I have seen God face to face, and yet my life has been spared."

This story also explains why it is that the Israelites do not eat the muscle of the hip, which is on the socket of the thigh, because the socket of Grabby's thigh was touched on the hip muscle in the fight with the stranger.

The Face of God

When Grabby looked down the long road ahead, he saw Hairy coming, accompanied by those four hundred men. So he divided the children among Leah, Rachel, and the two slave girls, and put the two slave girls and their children in front, with Leah and her children behind, and finally Rachel and Joseph at the rear. And he himself went on ahead of them to meet his brother.

Hairy ran to meet him, and threw his arms around him, and kissed him, and tears ran down Hairy's face, and tears ran down Grabby's face too. Then Hairy looked around and saw the women and the children, and he asked his brother, "What relation are all of these to you?"

To which Grabby replied, "These are the children whom God has graciously given me."

Then the women and children came up and paid homage to Hairy.

"What is the meaning of all of this company?" Hairy asked.

"To be perfectly frank, it is to win your favor," Grabby replied.

"Oh, I've got lots of stuff, my brother," Hairy said. "You just keep what you have."

Grabby said to him, "No, if I have found favor with you, accept my gifts, for to see your face is to see God's face, because you have treated me with mercy. Please take my gift. You have given me mercy. My gift is a small attempt to thank you."

So Hairy took the gift and said to his brother. "Let us now go south, and I will travel with you."

But crafty Grabby replied, "You can see that the children are little, and that I have all kinds of sheep and cattle that are very young. I don't want to over-drive them. You go on ahead, and I will proceed at a leisurely pace, and in due course, I will join you in the south."

"Let me assign some men to help you drive the animals," Hairy said.

"No," said Grabby, "you're too kind. We'll manage by ourselves."

And so Hairy started back that day for his own home, while Grabby followed along slowly toward the south. At Succoth he settled down for a while, building himself a house and sheds (Succoth) for his animals and that was how Succoth got its name.

No Way to Treat a Donkey

In spite of what he had promised his brother, Grabby did not continue his journey toward the south very long. Instead, he stopped at the city of Shechem, and for a price purchased a piece of ground near it, and there he settled down to live.

Now the ruler of the city of Shechem was a man whose name was Donkey, and he had a son whose name was Shechem. One day Dinah, Leah's daughter, went out to visit some of the women who lived in the area. When Shechem, Donkey's son, saw her, he grabbed her and raped her, because, as the story says he had a passionate longing for her.

Then he went to his father and said to him, "I'd like to marry that girl."

When Grabby heard that his daughter had been raped, he took no action, for his sons were far away working with the stock in the country. Before they returned, Donkey came to Grabby to talk to him, and while the two of them were talking, Dinah's brothers came in from the country. They heard what had happened, and were distressed and angry that such a thing had been done. But

Donkey said to them, "Look, my son Shechem really has his heart set on marrying your daughter. Would you please let him have her in marriage? You marry our women and we'll marry your women. You can settle down and live with us, and make your home here, and all of the land will be at your disposal. You can engage in trade with us, and play a regular role in our community."

And then Shechem, who was with his father, said to Grabby and to his sons, "If we find favor with you, I'd be happy to pay you anything you want for Dinah. Ask me any price you'd like, and I'll pay it. Just let me marry her."

The sons and the father thought over the proposal of Donkey and his son Shechem, and then they replied to them: "We cannot possibly let our sister marry a man who is outside of our group, a man who is uncircumcised. This would be a disgrace to us. But if you will be circumcised, and if all the males in your city will be circumcised, then we will let you have our sister. And we will let you marry our women, and we will marry yours, and we'll make our home here, and we'll become a single people. But if you will not agree to the proposal that we are making, then we will take our daughters and be off."

Donkey and his son thought the proposal over and agreed. Then they hurried back to the city of Shechem and summoned their fellow citizens to the city gate, where they said: "Grabby's sons are well disposed to us. Why not let them live here in our land and engage in trade with us, because this is a big land, and it's large enough to include them too. Let us enter into marriage contracts with them. They have agreed to do so, but they have agreed only on this one condition, that all of the men of the city be circumcised as they are. Don't you think it would be to our advantage to enter into such an agreement with them? If you do, then will you agree, all of you, to be circumcised?"

The men of the city of Shechem talked the whole proposal through, and after discussion they all agreed that they would be circumcised. Three days after the men of Shechem had been circumcised, when they had still not recovered from the operation, Simeon and Levi, Dinah's brothers, advanced on the city with their swords, and killed every last male in the city, including Donkey and his son Shechem. And they took Dinah out of Shechem's house and made off with her. The other brothers of

Dinah came into the city and sacked it and took its flocks and its herds and its donkeys, everything that was in the city, and everything that was in the field, and all of the wealth, and all of the women, and all of the children, and off they went.

When Grabby heard about it, he said to Simeon and Levi, "You fellows really shouldn't have done this. You're going to give us a bad reputation throughout the whole area."

It is obvious that the Lord's promises to Jacob are not made either because of his good character or his good intentions. They are strictly gratuitous. Moreover, it is equally clear that Jacob does not rest on these promises, nor does he make them the basis for his life. He lives as though God's promise did not also include a demand. He assumes that he has no responsibilities. Incredible as it may seem, in spite of the theophanies with their deeply moving words of grace, Jacob lives totally without reference to them. Even after the last wrestling match there is little more than a momentary change. Not even the "face of Esau" can change him. But God's love for Jacob is not daunted by his incapacity either to appropriate it or to appreciate it.

At the same time it ought not to be thought that Jacob escaped from his various escapades unscathed, as he was later to say to the Egyptian king, "My years have been few and hard. . . ." The fact is that for all of the successful deceit and skullduggery, Jacob's life was fraught with fear and loneliness. He left behind a shattered family—Isaac, Rebekah, and Esau. Laban was glad to be rid of him, and the ruins of the city of Shechem, while not directly his responsibility, remain mute witness to his sojourn there. Jacob's story is a sad story of what might have been, had his mother and he been more patient, and more prepared to let God work out his purposes in his own good time and in his own good way.

PART IV

Joseph
Man Proposes, God Disposes

It was von Rad's thesis that the Joseph story had distinct connections with the Wisdom tradition because Joseph is such a fine example of the personification of the Wisdom ideal. He is well-spoken, courteous, modest, learned, self-disciplined, calm and patient. His strength of character is legendary. So it is generally agreed that the figure of Joseph was drawn from the Wisdom tradition. But whereas Wisdom tends to be pragmatic in its goals with little to say about matters that are strictly theological, the Joseph story has a theological emphasis that is of primary importance. It is not, in short, a tractate on how to succeed in business or at the royal court. It is rather dedicated to the thesis that in his own inscrutable way God will effect this purpose, "that through you all the nations of the earth will be blessed," and that his purpose will not be circumvented by human behavior whether good or bad. But then, that has been the underlying thesis of the whole story up to this point.

Unlike the previous three sections of Genesis, the Joseph story is no longer, if it ever was, composed of discrete literary units, strung together like beads on a chain. As we have it today it is more of a polished literary whole through which one can still see the J and E sources but the seams between the two have been more carefully interwoven by the editors. It is their story that I propose to tell here rather than J's.

I
The Brothers

As a child Joseph was a precocious and pampered little dandy. Because he was the baby, and probably also because he was Rachel's child, his father favored him. In fact, his father went so far as to make a special tunic for him, much to the irritation of his older brothers whose animosity towards him increased as the days went by. Moreover, Joseph seems to have been totally oblivious to their feelings, for he was a dreamer of dreams, which he felt called upon to share with the rest of the family, although the meaning of the dreams was sufficiently obvious that one would not need to call in skilled analysts for help.

He said to them, "Listen to my dream: We were out binding sheaves in the field, when suddenly my sheaf stood up, and your sheaves gathered round and paid homage to my sheaf." His brothers figured that one out right away, and asked him, "Do you mean to rule over us?" He did not reply, and they drew their own conclusions.

He dreamed another dream, and told it too. "I've had another dream," he said, "and this time, the sun, and moon and eleven stars were bowing down to me." Even his father was a little perturbed by this dream, so he asked, "Are all of us, your mother, your brothers and I, to bow down to you?" Joseph did not answer. The father grew pensive. The brothers became angrier.

Some time later, when the brothers had gone off to pasture their father's sheep near Shechem, the old man sent Joseph to find out how things were going. He had difficulty finding them, but eventually located them with the help of a stranger. Unfortunately for him, they saw him coming, and easily recognized him because of his unique outfit. So they had time to plan a welcome for him. They said to one another, "Here comes the dreamer! Let's kill him, and throw his body into one of the pits, and say that an animal ate him!" Reuben succeeded in talking them out of killing him, and persuaded them to throw him into one of the nearby pits, because he had in mind to rescue him later. So they agreed to Reuben's suggestion. When Joseph came up to them, they grabbed him, stripped him of his fancy and offensive tunic, and threw him in the pit. Then they sat down to eat!

While they were eating, they saw an Ishmaelite caravan on its way to Egypt, and under Judah's influence they decided to sell him to the caravaneers. So they pulled him up out of the pit, and sold him to them for twenty pieces of silver, and the Ishmaelites took him off to Egypt. Then they slaughtered a little goat, and took his fancy tunic and dipped it in the blood, and brought the blood-stained tunic to his father, and said, "We found this. Is this your son's tunic?" He recognized it, of course, and was overcome with grief.

Meanwhile, the Ishmaelites sold Joseph into slavery in Egypt.

★ ★ ★ ★ ★

Was the Lord speaking through those dreams or were they just the idle fancies of a puffed-up little braggart? If they were divine revelations, then what is to happen to God's purpose? Has it been thwarted by the brothers' jealousy? If they were just Joseph's delusions of grandeur, did he get what he deserved? The reader is left with the questions, while the narrator takes us down another path.

II
Tamar

Now, for a moment, the record focuses on Judah. He has left his brothers, married a Canaanite woman, and has had three sons by her. The oldest of the sons grew up and married a woman named Tamar. When he died without having had children, it became the obligation of the remaining brothers to marry Tamar, and to have children by her in the name of the deceased. When the second brother died without their having had any children, and the duty now fell to the youngest brother, Judah said to Tamar, "You go and stay with your father until my son Shelah grows up," thus leaving Tamar with the notion that Judah still intended to see to the obligation owing to her late husband, although as a matter of fact, he had no such intention. So Tamar went home to her father.

Some years later Judah's wife died, and after the period of mourning was over he and a friend set our for Timnah to participate in the sheepshearing. When Tamar heard that he was on his way to Timnah, she took off her widow's clothes, dressed herself like a prostitute, put on a veil, and sat down alongside the Timnah road, for she had gradually come to the conclusion that he had no intention of carrying out his obligation either to her or to her dead husband. Along came Judah with his friend. He saw the attractive woman by the side of the road, did not recognize her because of the veil, and assumed that she was a prostitute. So he asked her if she would go to bed with him. She said, "What will you pay?" He said, "I'll send you a kid from the flock." She replied, "You've got to leave me some kind of a pledge." He said, "I'll leave my personal identification, my seal and cord, and my staff." So she said, "Give them to me." So he gave them to her, and off to bed they went. Afterward he went on to the sheepshearing with his friend, and she went home, and assumed her normal life, just a little bit pregnant.

When Judah's friend came back with the kid to redeem the pledge, she was nowhere to be found, and the townspeople knew nothing of a prostitute. So the friend brought the kid back to Judah. He explained the situation to him, and Judah decided that since he had tried to pay her, and had not been able to find her, he was no longer obligated, and that she could keep his seal and cord, and his staff, and he would just forget about it.

A few months later Judah got wind of a story that had been circulating to the effect that Tamar had been sleeping around, and that she was now pregnant. He was irate, of course, and demanded that she be burned as an adulteress. When they brought her out to burn her, she sent a message to Judah with his seal and cord, and staff, saying, "Take a look at these things. It's possible you might recognize them!" Needless to say, he did recognize them, and called off the burning, adding, "She is more in the right than I, inasmuch as I did not give her to my youngest son."

When the time came for her to give birth, she gave birth to twins whose names were Zerah and Perez.

★ ★ ★ ★ ★

The story of Judah and Tamar breaks the flow of the Joseph narrative, but it does serve some useful purposes in addition to giving the caravaneers time to get to Egypt! It gives us some inkling of the character of Judah who at a later point in the

Joseph story will play an extremely significant role, and will also display a sense of loyalty and familial devotion that contrasts with his behavior here. Perhaps he learned something from Tamar who certainly did have her priorities in order, and who might also have taught something about loyalty and fidelity to the lady who appears in the next episode.

Potiphar's Wife

In Egypt the Ishmaelites sold Joseph as a slave to a certain Potiphar, a royal courtier and chief steward of the Pharaoh, who took him home and put him to work. There Joseph became an immediate success, and not only because he was intelligent, hard-working, and quite devoted to his master, but also, and more importantly, *because the Lord was with him.* The more successful Joseph became, the more his master liked him, and the more he promoted him, until eventually he put Joseph in charge of the entire household, and made him his personal attendant. The more trust he put in Joseph, the more the Lord prospered him, so that eventually Potiphar left all the responsibilities of his estate to Joseph, and paid attention to nothing around the place but to what was put in front of him at mealtime.

So far, so good. It looked as though Joseph, with the Lord's help, was making very much the best of a bad situation when a new and a much greater threat arose in the person of Mrs. Potiphar. She had noticed that Joseph was a well-built, handsome fellow, and soon found herself very much attracted to him. When more subtle methods did not have the desired effect, she boldly propositioned him, only to have him turn her down on the grounds that he did not want to break his master's trust. He said, "He has given me full responsibility here. How could I do such a thing? It would be a sin against God!" But these words did not deflect her from her course.

One day Joseph came into the house to do his work. The servants were outside. Potiphar himself was out of town. So Mrs. Potiphar took this opportunity to take a more direct approach. She grabbed his tunic and said to him, "Come on to bed with me!" He pulled away from her. The tunic came off in her hand and he ran away. She began hollering and yelling, and when the servants rushed in, she said to them, "My husband brought this Hebrew here to make a mockery of us all. The fellow came in and tried to take advantage of me, but I started screaming, so he ran away leaving his tunic behind." When Potiphar came home, she showed him the tunic and told him the same story. He was furious and had Joseph put in prison, which was certainly a break for Joseph, for Potiphar might well have had him put to death.

In Jail

At first it was because of the envy and malice of his brothers that the Lord's plan for Joseph appeared to have gone astray, and then it was because of the lust and anger of Mrs. Potiphar. But as the old man said, "God moves in mischievous ways, his blunders to perform," and these incidents, which appear so unfair and so unfortunate, did not impede or even slow down the progress of God's purpose. On the contrary, the sale of Joseph into slavery and his incarceration in the jail only brought him that much closer to the place God intended that he should be. For in the jail the Lord continued to be with Joseph, so that in short order he became the chief jailer's favorite trustee. As it had been at the Potiphars', so it was now in the jail; nothing happened without Joseph's doing it, for the more Joseph was involved, the better things went, because the Lord was with him.

Some time later the royal cupbearer and the royal baker fell into disfavor with the king. They were put in custody, and became Joseph's wards. One night after they had been in the jail for a while, they both dreamed dreams. In the morning when Joseph came to them, he could see that they were upset. So he asked them why they were depressed. They explained that they had dreamed dreams, and that there was no one in the jail to interpret the dreams for them. To which Joseph replied, "Dream interpretations come from God, so tell them to me."

The chief cupbearer told his dream to Joseph first. He dreamed that he saw a vine with three branches. It budded, blossomed, and the clusters ripened into grapes, which he pressed into the royal cup, which he had in his hand. Then he took the cup to the king. Joseph explained to him that the dream meant that in three days the Pharaoh would pardon him, and would restore him to his former position. Then Joseph added, "Please don't forget me when he restores you. Please mention me to Pharaoh. I'd like to get out of here. I was kidnapped from my homeland, and I haven't done anything to deserve being in this place."

The chief baker was delighted with what Joseph had said to his colleague, so he hastened to set out his dream. He had dreamed that he was carrying three open baskets on his head. In the uppermost basket there were all kinds of baked good for the royal table, but the birds were eating out of the top basket. Joseph's interpretation of this dream was not as favorable. He said that the dream meant that in three days the king would cut off his head, and have his body impaled.

Sure enough, in three days Pharaoh made a banquet for all of the royal officials. At that time he restored the chief cupbearer to his position, but he had the chief baker executed.

In his euphoria however, the chief cupbearer forgot all about Joseph, who was left in the prison to cope with his disappointment as best he could.

Pharaoh's Dream

It was two years later that the chief butler remembered Joseph. Pharaoh had had two strange dreams, which the magicians and wise men of the royal court had not been able to interpret. In the first, he dreamed that he was standing by the Nile, and that up out of the river there came seven sleek, sturdy cows to graze by the river's edge. Right after them, there came up out of the Nile seven other cows, gaunt, wretched creatures who stood beside the first seven cows on the river bank. Then the seven ugly cows attacked the seven good ones and ate them up! At that Pharaoh awoke. After a while he went back to sleep and dreamed again. This time he dreamed of seven healthy ears of grain growing on a single stalk. Then up sprouted seven more ears of grain, thin and scorched by the desert wind. The seven thin ears swallowed up the seven full ears, and again his dream woke him up.

When no one was able to help the Pharaoh with his dreams, the chief cupbearer suddenly remembered Joseph. So he told the king of his experience in the jail. The king then sent for Joseph who was rushed from the jail, but not before he had changed his clothes, and had had his hair cut.

"I've had a dream," the king said, "and no one can interpret it. But I've heard it said that for you to hear a dream is to give its meaning."

Joseph replied. "It is not I but God who will see to Pharaoh's welfare."

When Pharaoh had spelled out his dreams, Joseph said to him, "The dreams are one and the same. God has told you what He is about to do. The seven healthy cows and the seven healthy ears of corn are seven years of great abundance in Egypt, which lie immediately ahead. The seven lean cows and the seven lean ears of grain are seven years of famine, during which all the abundance will be forgotten, for the famine will be very severe. And the reason for your having had the dream twice is that God has determined the matter, and will soon carry it out. So you need to find a skilled administrator and put him in charge of the land, and you need to set up an organizational structure immediately to collect the surplus during the good years that are coming, in order to have a reserve against the seven years of famine that will follow."

Both the Pharaoh and his courtiers were impressed with what Joseph had to say. After a brief discussion they agreed that he was the man for the job. So Pharaoh gave Joseph responsibility for all the land of Egypt. He put his signet ring on Joseph's hand; he dressed him in fine linen; he put a gold chain around his neck;

and he had him ride around in a chariot as second-in-command in all the land of Egypt. Then Pharaoh signaled Joseph's acceptance in Egyptian court circles by giving him an Egyptian name, and by having him marry the daughter of the high priest at Heliopolis, who bore him two sons, Manasseh and Ephraim.

Cat and Mouse

During the seven years of plenty, Joseph worked hard at preparing stockpiles of grain for the years of famine that were imminent. And as he had predicted, when the years of plenty were over, the seven years of famine set in. There was famine everywhere in the world except in Egypt. So now in a first fulfillment of the promise made to Abraham many years before, all the families of the earth came to Egypt to be blessed with food through the work of Joseph.

Canaan, of course, did not escape the famine, and when Jacob discovered that there was grain in Egypt, he said to his sons, "Why are you standing here looking at one another? There's grain in Egypt. Go down and get some for us before we starve to death." So ten of Joseph's brothers set off for Egypt to get grain, but Jacob kept Benjamin, Joseph's younger full brother, at home, lest something should happen to him.

Now to get grain in Egypt one had to approach Joseph directly, and so it was that the ten brothers eventually came before him, and bowed down to him with their faces to the ground. Joseph recognized them immediately, and remembered his earlier dream as well. But they did not recognize him. So he decided to play a game of cat and mouse with them.

"Where are you from?" he asked.

"We came from Canaan to buy food," they answered.

"You look to me like spies," he said.

"Oh, no, sir," they said. "Your servants really have come just to buy food. We're honest men. We're brothers. We've never been spies."

"No," he said, "you're spies."

Pathetically, they replied, "We were twelve brothers of a certain man in Canaan. The youngest stayed at home with his father, and the other is no more."

But Joseph said, "It's just what I said. You're spies! We'll test the truth of what you say. If your younger brother doesn't come down here, then I swear by the king that you'll never leave here. So one of you go and get your younger brother, and the rest of you stay confined here until we find out whether you're telling the truth or not." So he locked them up for three days.

On the third day Joseph said to them, "I'm going to give you a break because I am a religious man. I'm going to detain one of your brothers here, and let the rest of you go home with grain for your families. But if you're going to live, you must bring me back your youngest brother in order to prove that you were telling the truth." They had no choice but to agree, although they did so reluctantly, and with a strong sense that at long last they were about to face the consequences of their ill-treatment of Joseph. Reuben also did not lose the opportunity of chiding them for not paying attention to him. "Didn't I tell you?" he said. Didn't I tell you not to hurt him? But you wouldn't pay any attention. Now look where we are."

Joseph had been speaking to them through an interpreter so they had no idea that he understood what they were saying. Hence they spoke more freely than they might otherwise have done. He was touched enough by their anxiety and their uncertainty to weep, but not enough to stop tormenting them. He took Simeon and had him tied up right in front of them. Then he gave orders to fill their bags with grain and to return each man's money to his sack. Then they were given provisions for their journey and off they went.

That night one of them opened his sack to get some grain to feed his donkey and saw his money right there in the mouth of the sack. "My money has been returned," he said to his brothers. "It's right here in my bag!" Their hearts sank. Trembling, they turned to one another and said, "What in the world has God done to us?"

When they got back to Canaan, they told their father everything that had happened in Egypt; how the man had accused them of being spies; how they had tried to defend themselves by explaining their family history; how finally he had insisted on keeping Simeon as surety, and how, on sending them off he had warned them that Simeon would never get out, and that they'd never get any more grain unless they brought

Benjamin back to Egypt to verify the truth of their story. Then they started to empty their sacks only discover to their great dismay that each man's money was in his sack. With that discovery the father began to berate them. "You're always bereaving me," he said. "First it was Joseph. Now it's Simeon. Next it'll be Benjamin! Everything always happens to me!" Reuben tried to comfort his father by saying, "Trust him to me. He'll be safe with me. You can kill both of my sons if I don't bring him back to you." But Jacob would not be comforted. "He can't go," he said. "His brother is dead. He's the only one I've got left. If anything were to happen to him, I would die."

The Second Visit

There was no sign of relief from the famine so that the day came all too soon when Jacob said to his sons, "Go back to Egypt and get us some more grain." Judah said to his father, "The man told us not to come anywhere near him without Benjamin. If you'll let Benjamin come with us, we'll go down there to see what we can get, but if you won't let him come, we won't go, because it would be pointless." The old man said, "Why did you have to tell him you had another brother?" And they said, "Because he kept asking us questions about our family: Is your father still alive? Do you have another brother? How were we supposed to know that he would say, 'Bring your brother down here'?"

Finally Judah said to his father, "I'll take the responsibility for him. Send him with me. If I don't bring him back to you, and set him down right here in front of you, you can hold me eternally responsible. We could have been down there and back twice, if it hadn't been for all of this arguing."

Reluctantly the old man said, "If it must be, it must be. But at least do this: take the man some of the best products of the land as a gift, a little balm, a little honey, some gum, some myrrh, some pistachio nuts and some almonds. And take back the money. Maybe that was a mistake. Take Benjamin too and hurry." Then with a brief prayer to El Shaddai for mercy, he sent them back to Egypt.

So they made their way to Egypt and presented themselves to Joseph. When he saw Benjamin, he ordered his steward to take them home, and to prepare for them to eat with him at noon. This was unusual behavior, and aroused their suspicion. They couldn't figure out why he would bother with them unless he had some evil scheme in mind like taking them into slavery because of the money's being replaced in their sacks. So they approached the steward apprehensively, and tried to explain about the money. "We came down here before, sir," they said, "and we bought grain. But the first night on our way home we found our money in our sacks. So we have brought the money back with some more to buy food. We don't know how the money got there." He replied, "Everything is OK. Your account is paid. You don't need to be afraid. Perhaps your God put your money in your bags!" Then he brought out Simeon, and he got some water for them to bathe their feet, and they laid out their gifts in preparation for Joseph's coming.

When Joseph got home, they presented their gifts and did a lot of obsequious bowing and scraping. He asked about his father, and while they were replying, he was able to keep his composure until he saw Benjamin. At that point his emotions almost overcame him, but he did struggle successfully with them until he got out of the room. After some lonely tears he washed his face, reappeared, and gave the order to serve the meal. That he ate by himself did not surprise them, for Egyptians do not eat with foreigners, but what was astonishing was that they were seated in order, from the oldest to the youngest, at his direction!

When the meal was over, Joseph ordered his steward to prepare them for their return journey, to fill their bags with grain, to put each one's money back in his bag, and to put in the mouth of Benjamin's bag Joseph's silver goblet. The following morning the brothers were sent off with their animals. They had hardly got out of the city before Joseph sent his steward after them to accuse them of stealing his divination cup.

When the steward overtook them, and asked them why they had stolen the cup, they were astounded, and replied, "How can you say such a thing? We wouldn't do anything like that! We even brought the money back that we found in our bags. How could you even imagine that we would steal silver or gold from your master's house? If any one of us is guilty, you can put him to death, and the rest of us will become your slaves!" The steward replied that he was looking only for the one who was guilty, and that the rest could go free.

So they put their bags down on the ground, and the search began, proceeding from the oldest to the youngest. Bag after bag was opened until the goblet turned up in Benjamin's bag. One can easily imagine their frustration and anxiety as they tore their clothes in grief, reloaded their pack animals, and returned to the city.

When they got to Joseph's house, they prostrated themselves on the ground before him, and he said to them, "What were you trying to do?" Judah's response was, "What can we say? How can we prove our innocence? God has exposed us for what we are. So we'll be your slave, all of us, and not just Benjamin who had the goblet." But Joseph said, "No! I only want the one who had the goblet. The rest of you may go."

Then Judah, the one whose idea it was to sell him into slavery in the first place, approached Joseph and said to him, "Please, sir, don't be impatient with your servant, but I must appeal to you. You were the one who asked us whether we had a father or another brother, and we told you that we had an aged father with a son of his old age whose full brother was dead, so that his father doted on him. Then you said, 'Bring him down here. I want to see him.' We told you then that it was impossible because if the boy were to leave him, his father would die. But you told us that if we could not bring him, not to come anywhere near you. We explained all of this to our father when we got home, and his response was that if anything were to happen to Benjamin, he would die. Now if we go home and the boy is not with us, he will die, and we will be responsible for killing him. Sir, I pledged myself to my father for the boy that I would bring him back or be eternally guilty. So now, please, let me stay as your slave instead of the boy, and let him go back with his brothers. How could I go back to my father without him? I wouldn't want to see my father's suffering."

Judah's words touched Joseph so deeply that he could no longer control himself, so he ordered his Egyptian attendants to leave, and with sobs he revealed himself to his brothers. They didn't know what to say. So he said to them, "Come close to me. I'm your brother Joseph whom you sold into Egypt. Don't be upset, and don't feel guilty, for it was to save life that God sent me here ahead of you. It was to insure your survival, and to save your lives in an extraordinary way. It was not you who sent me here. It was God. And He has made me father to Pharaoh, lord of his household, and ruler over the whole land. Hurry back to my father, and tell him what God has done, and tell him about me, and bring him back here with your families, that I may provide for all of you for the next five years of famine, that you may not suffer again." Then Joseph hugged and kissed them all with tears and great excitement. The brothers, however, said very little.

When Pharaoh heard the news that Joseph's brothers had come, he supported Joseph's enthusiastic invitation to them. He sent them back to Canaan loaded with gifts, and with instructions to bring their father and their families back to the security of Egypt.

Conclusion

Jacob quickly overcame his initial shock at the news that Joseph was not only still alive but that he had achieved such a lofty position in Egypt. He went to the Beersheba shrine to offer the Lord sacrifices, and there God appeared to him, sanctioning his visit to Egypt and affirming that it was a part of the divine plan and purpose. So Jacob went to Egypt to be warmly greeted by Joseph and the Pharaoh. He and his sons settled with their flocks and families in the land of Goshen.

The famine by that time was even more severe. Everyone in both Egypt and Canaan was utterly dependent upon Joseph's rationing system. Soon Joseph had gathered into the Pharaoh's coffers all of the money in both Egypt and Canaan. When their money ran out, the people had to barter their livestock, and then their land for grain. Ultimately, therefore, all the land in Egypt except that belonging to the religious shrines passed into the possession of the Pharaoh. So Joseph made a land law in Egypt that would be applicable when the famine was over, that one-fifth of all the seed should go to Pharaoh. And that law is still valid to this day.

When the time came for Jacob to die, he made Joseph promise him that he would take him back to Canaan to bury him with his fathers near Mamre. So after his death Joseph took Jacob back to Canaan and buried him in accordance with his request.

When the brothers saw that their father was dead, they were very much concerned that Joseph might now seek vengeance. So they sent this message to Joseph: "Before his death your father told us to tell you to forgive us for the way we treated you. So please forgive us." Then they went to him directly and said. "We're ready to be your slaves."

But Joseph said to them, "You do not need to be afraid. You intended to do me harm but God intended that good should come from your act—that many people should have life. So do not be afraid. I will support you and your children."

NOTES

NOTES

NOTES